Please return to:
Ruth Allison
630 772741f
6699 Edwards
Holland, MI
49423

Praise for *Help Is Here*

"Never before has a book so beautifully invited me to sit down, take a breath, and unpack the overwhelm, exhaustion, and burnout that's underscored the last few years. Max's works always feel like coffee with a dear friend, but *Help Is Here* is different. Max's latest book challenges us to fight for a new way ahead—trusting in our Savior to not just nudge us from the darkness but to rescue us and lead us in Glory. Max's words are poetic and pointed—steeped in Grace and rooted in scripture. This is a must-read for anyone who's been through the ringer and ready for a new way."

—Emily Ley, bestselling author and founder of Simplified

"Do you want to have a deeper, closer relationship with God? You can do that through the Holy Spirit! In my good friend Max Lucado's new book, *Help Is Here*, he explores the person, power, and provision of the Holy Spirit. Max explains how having a relationship with Him makes your life fuller, richer, and more exciting than you ever dreamed possible. You must read this book!"

—Robert Morris, senior pastor, Gateway Church; bestselling author
of *The Blessed Life*, *Beyond Blessed*, and *Take the Day Off*

"Max's leadership and beautiful testimonies throughout these pages have encouraged and equipped me in how to embrace the Holy Spirit and choose praise instead of panic. Through his stories and deep knowledge, Max lovingly reminds us that worship and praise are the answers for our anxiety-ridden, overworked, and overstressed pace of life."

—Hillary Scott Tyrell, Grammy Award–winning co-lead singer of Lady A

"For years I have longed as a pastor for a book like this on my shelf to give away. Finally, not a doctrine or an explanation of the Holy Spirit, but an actual introduction and invitation to God's living presence."

—Richard Kannwischer, senior pastor at Peachtree Presbyterian Church

"Are you weary? Burned out? Simply dissatisfied with your spiritual life? Let my friend Max Lucado tell you all about your Helper—the divine Spirit who changes everything. This exhilarating book—both profound and practical—will energize your life with God as never before. Don't miss the life-changing adventure that's inside these pages!"

—Lee Strobel, bestselling author of *The Case
for Christ* and *The Case for Heaven*

"Max Lucado's brilliant mind and tender heart are on display once again in his newest book, *Help Is Here*. Max combines his renowned storytelling with powerful, biblical revelation about the person of the Holy Spirit. This is a beautiful and important book. Nothing stretches the imagination more than recognizing that God gives Himself to us as an inheritance. The person of the Holy Spirit is our greatest gift, and it is our delight to learn how to host Him well. Everything true, noble, and beautiful in us comes from the Father, who filled us with His Spirit, empowering us to do what was humanly impossible. We have been called to be, as Max writes, 'the supernatural expression of God on the planet.' What a privilege; what a responsibility; what a joy."

—Bill Johnson, Bethel Church, Redding, California; author
of *Open Heavens* and *Born for Significance*

"Few people in the evangelical world write with the penetrating insight and persuasive clarity as does my friend Max Lucado. This book testifies to that once again. When Max first informed me that he was writing a book on the Holy Spirit, I knew in an instant the impact it would have. Many who have followed Max's ministry through the years will be surprised when they discover that he now believes in the contemporary validity of all spiritual gifts in the life of the church today. Max's thoroughly biblical case for the work of the Spirit will challenge and, ultimately, persuade you of its truth, and greatly encourage you to seek for an even greater manifestation of the Spirit's power in your life. I highly and happily recommend it."

—Sam Storms, Ph.D., Enjoying God Ministries, author
of *Understanding Spiritual Gifts: A Comprehensive Guide*

"Max Lucado possesses a miraculous ability to distill the deep waters of God into refreshing springs of simplicity and grace. We couldn't imagine walking out the purposes of God in our lives without the empowering understanding of the Holy Spirit that Max's new book provides. If you've ever wondered how it's possible to navigate the challenges of this world and still 'consider it all joy,' *Help Is Here* is not to be missed!"

—Matt and Lauri Crouch, Trinity Broadcasting Network

"In our heaviest times, *Help Is Here* shines a bright light of hope and encouragement to show us that no matter what we go through, we do not have to carry the burdens alone. Whether it's hardship or burnout, Max Lucado reminds us there is help, and it's not far away but ever-present in times of trouble."

—Sadie Robertson Huff, bestselling author,
speaker, and founder of Live Original

"Max Lucado is not only a hugely talented writer, he also has insights into spiritual truths which draw us all closer to Jesus."

—Nicky Gumbel, pioneer of Alpha

"The Holy Spirit . . . the most misunderstood, misrepresented member of the Trinity—and yet, before Jesus ascended into heaven He told his disciples not to leave Jerusalem until the Holy Spirit had come upon them. The promise was that they would receive power from on high. Who doesn't want that? Who doesn't need that? Let Max walk you through the amazing scriptures that describe the wonder, the promise, and the power of the Holy Spirit, who is available and so necessary for each and every one of us who follow Jesus. Thank you, Max . . . we needed this!"

—Terry Meeuwsen, cohost, *The 700 Club*; founder, Orphan's Promise

"Max Lucado's honoring of Jesus' Free Gift of the Holy Spirit to every Christian believer, apart from any deserving preconditions or 'surrenderings' whatsoever in order to 'deserve' this Spirit, is full of encouragements to be simply and daily alive to this Indwelling One! I warmly recommend Lucado's wise counsel."

—Dr. Frederick Dale Bruner, Professor of Theology
   Emeritus, Whitworth University

"Reading the Bible, prayer, church, time spent away from the endless scroll of social media and 24/7 news . . . A life of peace is not out of reach but, as it's been said, the easy things to do are also easy not to do. Our culture grows more anxious, more stressed, and more hopeless by the minute all the while the things that make for peace sit idly by. If you've been left feeling increasingly helpless or debilitated by despair, let Max Lucado gently steer you to greener pastures. The practical help and hope found in *Help Is Here* will put heaven's wind at your back and give you the tools to reclaim your confidence."

—Levi Lusko, lead pastor of Fresh Life Church and bestselling author

"Lucado offers a lifeline for every weary person on the planet. Read. Inhale the breath of Life. Know the joy and power from above."

—Ken Shigematsu, pastor of Tenth Church, Vancouver,
   BC; bestselling author of *God in My Everything*

ALSO BY MAX LUCADO

INSPIRATIONAL
3:16
A Gentle Thunder
A Love Worth Giving
And the Angels Were Silent
Anxious for Nothing
Because of Bethlehem
Before Amen
Come Thirsty
Cure for the Common Life
Facing Your Giants
Fearless
Glory Days
God Came Near
Grace
Great Day Every Day
He Chose the Nails
He Still Moves Stones
How Happiness Happens
In the Eye of the Storm
In the Grip of Grace
It's Not About Me
Just Like Jesus
Max on Life
More to Your Story
Next Door Savior
No Wonder They Call
  Him the Savior
On the Anvil
Outlive Your Life
Six Hours One Friday
The Applause of Heaven
The Great House of God
Traveling Light
Unshakable Hope
When Christ Comes
When God Whispers
  Your Name
You Are Never Alone
You'll Get Through This
You Were Made for
  This Moment

COMPILATIONS
Begin Again
Jesus
Start with Prayer
They Walked with God

FICTION
Christmas Stories
Miracle at the Higher
  Grounds Café
The Christmas Candle

BIBLES (GENERAL EDITOR)
Children's Daily
  Devotional Bible
Grace for the Moment
  Daily Bible
The Lucado Encouraging
  Word Bible
The Lucado Life
  Lessons Study Bible

CHILDREN'S BOOKS
A Max Lucado
  Children's Treasury
Do You Know I
  Love You, God?
God Always Keeps
  His Promises
God Forgives Me,
  and I Forgive You
God Listens When I Pray
Grace for the Moment:
  365 Devotions for Kids
Hermie, a Common
  Caterpillar
I'm Not a Scaredy Cat
Itsy Bitsy Christmas
Just in Case You
  Ever Wonder

Lucado Treasury of
  Bedtime Prayers
One Hand, Two Hands
Thank You, God,
  for Blessing Me
Thank You, God,
  for Loving Me
The Boy and the Ocean
The Crippled Lamb
The Oak Inside the Acorn
The Tallest of Smalls
Where'd My Giggle Go?
You Are Mine
You Are Special

YOUNG ADULT BOOKS
3:16
It's Not About Me
Make Every Day Count
Wild Grace
You Were Made to
  Make a Difference

GIFT BOOKS
Fear Not Promise Book
For the Tough Times
God Thinks You're
  Wonderful
Grace for the Moment
Grace Happens Here
Happy Today
His Name Is Jesus
Let the Journey Begin
Live Loved
Mocha with Max
Safe in the Shepherd's Arms
This Is Love
You Changed My Life

Help Is Here

Finding Fresh Strength and Purpose
in the Power of the Holy Spirit

MAX LUCADO

THOMAS NELSON
Since 1798

Published in Nashville, Tennessee, by Thomas Nelson. Thomas Nelson is a registered trademark of HarperCollins Christian Publishing, Inc.

Thomas Nelson titles may be purchased in bulk for educational, business, fund-raising, or sales promotional use. For information, please e-mail SpecialMarkets@ThomasNelson.com.

Any Internet addresses, phone numbers, or company or product information printed in this book are offered as a resource and are not intended in any way to be or to imply an endorsement by Thomas Nelson, nor does Thomas Nelson vouch for the existence, content, or services of these sites, phone numbers, companies, or products beyond the life of this book.

Unless otherwise noted, Scripture quotations are taken from The Holy Bible, English Standard Version®, copyright © 2001 by Crossway, a publishing ministry of Good News Publishers. Used by permission. All rights reserved

Other scriptures are from the following sources: Amplified® Bible (AMP), copyright © 1954, 1958, 1962, 1964, 1965, 1987 by The Lockman Foundation. Used by permission. (www. Lockman.org). Amplified Bible, Classic Edition (AMPC). Good News Translation in Today's English Version—Second Edition (GNT). © 1992 by American Bible Society. Holy Bible: International Standard Version (ISV), © 1995–2014. King James Version (KJV).The Message (THE MESSAGE). Copyright © by Eugene H. Peterson 1993, 1994, 1995, 1996, 2000, 2001, 2002. Used by permission of Tyndale House Publishers, Inc. New American Standard Bible® (NASB). Copyright © 1960, 1962, 1963, 1968, 1971, 1972, 1973, 1975, 1977, 1995 by The Lockman Foundation. Used by permission. (www.Lockman.org). New Century Version® (NCV). © 2005 by Thomas Nelson. Used by permission. All rights reserved. New English Bible (NEB). Cambridge University Press and Oxford University Press 1961, 1970. All rights reserved. Holy Bible, New International Version®, NIV® (NIV). Copyright © 1973, 1978, 1984, 2011 by Biblica, Inc.™ Used by permission of Zondervan. All rights reserved worldwide. www.zondervan.com. New King James Version® (NKJV). © 1982 by Thomas Nelson. Used by permission. All rights reserved. Holy Bible, New Living Translation (NLT). © 1996, 2004, 2007, 2013, 2015 by Tyndale House Foundation. Used by permission of Tyndale House Publishers, Inc., Carol Stream, IL 60188. All rights reserved. New Revised Standard Version Bible (NRSV). © 1989 National Council of the Churches of Christ in the United States of America. Used by permission. All rights reserved. J. B. Phillips: THE NEW TESTAMENT IN MODERN ENGLISH, Revised Edition (PHILLIPS). © J. B. Phillips 1958, 1960, 1972. Used by permission of Macmillan Publishing Co., Inc. The Living Bible (TLB). Copyright © 1971. Used by permission of Tyndale House Publishers, Inc., Carol Stream, Illinois 60188. All rights reserved.

ISBN: 978-1-4002-2481-4 (HC)
ISBN: 978-1-4002-3002-0 (IE)
ISBN: 978-1-4002-2482-1 (eBook)
ISBN: 978-1-4041-1855-3 (custom)

Library of Congress Cataloging-in-Publication Data

Names: Lucado, Max, author.
Title: Help is here : finding fresh strength and purpose in the power of the
    holy spirit / Max Lucado.
Description: Nashville, Tennessee : Thomas Nelson, 2022. | Includes
    bibliographical references.
Identifiers: LCCN 2020040769 (print) | LCCN 2020040768 (ebook) | ISBN
    9781400224814 (hardcover) | ISBN 9781400224821 (epub) | ISBN
    9781400224821(epub) | ISBN 9781400224814(hardcover)
Subjects: LCSH: Holy Spirit.
Classification: LCC BT121.3 .L835 2021 (ebook) | LCC BT121.3 (print) | DDC
    231/.3--dc23
LC record available at https://lccn.loc.gov/2020040769

Printed in the United States of America

22 23 24 25 26 LSC 6 5 4 3 2 1

It is the Spirit who gives life; the flesh is no help at all.
—Jesus (John 6:63)

With great joy I dedicate this book to
Dr. Pete Ledoux
Child of our good Father, lover of the Spirit,
follower of Jesus, and servant of people.

Contents

Acknowledgments

If only you could meet the phenomenal team behind this book. They are steadfast, creative, and dedicated. Thanks to them, chapters are completed, covers are designed, books are distributed, and lives are touched. If publishing had a Hall of Fame, these folks, without exception, would be in it.

Liz Heaney and Karen Hill—editors extraordinaire. There is nothing easy about prodding this stubborn mule of an author. They clarify, disentangle, and correct. And they have done so for thirty years!

Carol Bartley—How many grammatical errors, misquotes, and fumbles have you fixed? You are to a manuscript what a dentist is to a mouth of cavities. Thanks for the extractions.

David Drury—Your expertise and intellect have spared me from crucial mistakes. Thank you for reviewing this work.

Steve and Cheryl Green—Lifelong friends and devoted servants.

The HCCP team of superheroes—Mark Schoenwald, Don Jacobson, Tim Paulson, Mark Glesne, Erica Smith, Janene MacIvor, and Laura Minchew.

Greg and Susan Ligon—If you ever choose to run for president, you get my vote. You can keep a train on the track like none other.

Andrea Lucado—Your great work on the "Questions for Reflection" made this Papa proud.

Dave Treat—Once again you lifted up this project in prayer. May your highest prayers be answered.

Caroline Green—Welcome to this team! We are blessed to have you.

Jana Muntsinger and Pamela McClure—You smooth over the rocky road of publicity. Thanks to you, doors are opened and the word gets out.

Joy Pruett—Thank you for your careful reading of the early draft and for your valuable feedback.

Janie Padilla and Margaret Mechinus—Ever steady, quiet, and rock solid. Thank you.

Brett, Jenna, Rosie, Max, Andrea, Jeff, and Sara—No Papa could be prouder of his family than I am of you.

Denalyn, my bride—The writing of this book coincided with our fortieth year of marriage. Forty years! Forty minutes is more like it. I love you, and I want you to know I would do it all again.

And to you, the reader—Blessings on you! I am so honored that you would entrust me with a few minutes of your time. I do not take the privilege lightly. Be equally assured I'm aware of my limited understanding. To ponder the Spirit is to ponder an endless ocean of beauty. No one comprehends the depths. The words of Bernard Ramm are spot-on:

> There is a hiddenness to the Spirit that cannot be uncovered. There is
> an immediacy of the Spirit that cannot be shoved into vision. There

is an invisibility of the Spirit that cannot be forced into visibility. There is a reticence of the Spirit that cannot be converted into openness. For these reasons one feels helpless, inadequate, and unworthy to write a line about the Spirit.[1]

The Spirit defies comprehension yet welcomes the attempt. This is mine. May it encourage you.

Preface

Let's imagine you're on a vacation. You load the car and drive to a mountain village hotel. Clean air. Splendid vistas. Cool weather. It's going to be great. Besides, this hotel is offering an end-of-season special that fits your budget. This is your chance to do what you've always wanted to do: hike the mountain trails.

On the first morning you're the first person out the door. No sleeping in for you, no sirree. Pack on back. Water bottle full and enthusiasm level high. Trail map in one hand, walking stick in the other. What fun!

The fun is short lived. The trail is steep. Your new hiking boots are stiff. A few minutes up the trail you wonder, *Did someone stuff sandbags in my backpack?*

You step to the side of the path to catch your breath. That's when you hear the trail guide and his happy followers. He wears a wide-brimmed hat and speaks with a confident tone that makes you think he knows his stuff. He identifies the names of the flowers, describes the history of the trail, and shares a few tips on the best way to have the best day of hiking.

His followers aren't carrying gear, so they walk at a fast clip. The guide points out wildlife along the way and pauses to answer the hikers' questions. You consider tagging along and eavesdropping. But you didn't pay for a guide. Besides, you couldn't keep up.

Within moments the group is way ahead. You lag behind with your increasingly uncomfortable load.

After a few miles you catch up. They are sitting in a meadow, listening to the guide describe the vast mountain range. And they are eating lunch! Sandwiches, chips, sodas, and cookies. Are those homemade chocolate chip cookies? It's a feast!

You sigh and wonder if the PB&J you brought is going to be soggy. No matter. You've lost your appetite. You turn and head down the trail. Enough misery for a day.

The next morning your muscles ache and your feet are swollen. It takes the better part of an hour and a box of Band-Aids to cover your blisters. Off you go to try a different trail. Day two is a mirror image of day one. The trail is steep too soon. Your legs are tired too fast, and if the backpack felt full of sandbags yesterday, today it feels as though it contains concrete blocks.

And guess who you hear coming up the trail behind you? That's right. The cheerful guide and his gaggle of fortunate followers. You step to the side of the trail and let them pass. One of them is whistling. A couple are chatting. The guide makes a joke, and the others laugh.

And you? Think arthritic pack mule.

Within a few miles you come upon the group again. They are, you guessed it, sitting in a meadow, eating a picnic lunch, enjoying a nature presentation.

"We have homemade ice cream," the guide announces. "Let's eat it up!"

You grumble something about the inequities of life, turn around, and walk back to the hotel. You spend the afternoon watching reality TV and eating your PB&J.

Days three and four? Identical to days one and two.

On day five you don't even leave the hotel lobby.

You are minding your own business when you hear someone call your name. You look up. It is the hiking guide.

"I've been looking for you," he says. "Where have you been?"

"What?"

"I've been hoping you would be a part of our daily hikes. They are included in your package. The lectures. The food. It's all a part of the deal. Maybe you didn't read the brochure we sent."

"I guess I didn't."

"We take care of everything. We truck your pack up the trail so you don't have to carry it. We have a team that prepares a gourmet meal. And, well, you get *me*. I know these trails better than anyone. My job is to lead you into the high country."

"Really? How did I miss that?"

ℓℓ

There is a weariness among us. We are weary from the loads we carry and the challenges we face. We have questions we cannot answer and problems we cannot solve. We'd hoped that life would be an invigorating pilgrimage, a high-country adventure. We never expected to grow so tired so soon.

We grow weary on the walk.

Yet what if there is help? Someone to walk with you and guide you, to shoulder the load.

And what if this help was heaven-sent? Not another person who, like you, is prone to blisters and leg cramps. Someone who is ever strong. Never tires. Always near. Unhindered by what hinders us.

Interested?

Pack away the Band-Aids and PB&Js. No more blisters for you, my friend. A better climb awaits.

CHAPTER 1

The Holy Who?

We have not even heard that there is a Holy Spirit.
—Acts 19:2

And now I will send the Holy Spirit upon you, just as my Father promised. Don't begin telling others yet—stay here in the city until the Holy Spirit comes and fills you with power from heaven.
—Luke 24:49 TLB

I began attending church as a youngster. Gung ho and willing to tackle the mountain, I was barely into double-digit years before I was reading my Bible, memorizing scriptures, and doing my dead-level best to obey every command I heard from the pulpit. I hoisted the backpack of good Christian living and set out to scale the lofty peaks of morality, spirituality, and devotion.

Always tell the truth.

Never lag in faith.

Pray more.

Do more.

Believe more.

Believe me, I tried. But, boy, did that trail grow steep. Peer pressure, raging hormones, and guilt conspired to convince me I'd never make it. Can a fifteen-year-old suffer spiritual burnout? This one did.

Maybe you know the feeling.

The fire in your belly is running low on kindling. But where is the firewood?

It's not for lack of searching. The Lord knows you've tried. At least you hope he knows. You've signed up and stood up for everything you know to be right and good. Yet why this cold wind in the face? Why this uphill struggle? These gray skies? This empty spot?

Something's missing, and for the life of you the life of you feels as if it is fading.

Drip by drip. Little by little. Day by day.

If that is you, can we talk? Can we start with this? The Lord does know. He does care. It is not his will that you lead a lifeless life. He has something—no, Someone—you need to know.

I do not recall being told about this source of strength. I don't fault anyone. After all, I owned a Bible. I could have searched the pages. Yet had you asked me to explain him to you, I would've just shrugged and said, "The Holy Who?"

Ask people, *"Who is God the Father?"* They have a ready reply. Or *"Describe God the Son."* Most will not hesitate to answer. But if you want to see someone hem, haw, and search for words, ask, *"Who is the Holy Spirit?"*

Part of the challenge is found in the terms. God as *Father*? We comprehend that image.

God as Jesus, the *Son*? That idea is manageable as well.

But God as *Spirit*? The word itself is mystical.

I do recall an early encounter with him.[1] I was wrapping up my senior year of high school when a wonderful thing happened in our small West Texas town. An evangelist from a far-off country called California showed up in a school bus that had been painted to look like a flower garden. He was a convert in the Jesus Movement that was sweeping the country in the early 1970s. He wore shoulder-length hair and bell-bottom jeans. He set up camp in the school parking lot and began preaching about Christ and the power of the Spirit. By that time in my life, I'd abandoned the steep mountain trail of spirituality. The only spirit I knew came in the form of a liquor store bottle. The hippie preacher invited a group of us to attend a Bible study in homes and learn more. So I went to one.

The address I was given took me to a trailer house on the edge of town. I didn't know anyone there, but everyone was very kind. We sat on the floor, read from the book of Acts, and for the first time that I can recall, I heard someone describe the work of the Holy Spirit. The exact words I've long since forgotten. But the sentiment I readily remember: The Spirit is your life-giving friend, here to lead you home.

> The Spirit is your life-giving friend, here to lead you home.

When we prayed, a couple of people prayed in a language I'd never heard. They asked if I'd like to pray in the same manner. I said, "Yes." I tried, but nothing happened. Even so, I was impressed. These people didn't seem trail weary. They were invigorated. Their eyes lit up when they spoke about the Spirit.

You might expect my story to take a dramatic turn at this point. A Damascus road moment, perhaps. Saul becoming Paul. But, alas, there was no bright light in the trailer park. I didn't become an apostle or write epistles. Quite the contrary. I was so convinced that I was unqualified to walk with the Spirit, I didn't even try.

More years of prodigal living ensued. The pigpen became my home address, and the other pigs were my tribe. Worse still, I continued to call myself a Christian, hopping nightclubs on Saturday nights, sitting in a pew on Sunday mornings. I was the hypocrite who turns others away from Christ.

In my early twenties a dear man, who eventually became a dear friend, helped me believe that God's grace was greater than my rebellion. I knelt at a church altar, trusted heaven's mercy, and set out on the trail again. Forgiveness became my message, my life story. I changed my career path, went through seminary, and served churches in Miami and Rio de Janeiro and eventually settled down as a pastor in San Antonio, Texas.

That's where the wheels came off again.

If you think the trail of Christian living is steep for a youngster, it is even more so for a minister. I resolved to study hard, counsel wisely, solve problems, organize committees, and satisfy each cranky member. I maintained a game face for three or four years, but somewhere in my midthirties I ran out of fuel. Suddenly I could not sleep. How does a person lose the ability to sleep? I'd climb into bed and listen to the relaxed breathing of my wife. I'd imagine my three young daughters snoozing in their beds down the hall. I'd think about my friends and coworkers, each of whom was resting peacefully. Our dog was sleeping. Our goldfish was sleeping.

And me? My mind was racing, a Ferrari on a time trial. I thought of members to be called, decisions to be made. On more than one Sunday morning, I stood before the church having had little, if any, sleep. I was desperate.

Was this the season in which I found the Holy Spirit? Sort of. It would be more accurate to say the Spirit found me.

In those late-night hours when I could not sleep, I would climb out of bed, pad down the stairs, and kneel at our couch and pray. Dejected figure I was. Not Max the pastor. Not Max the church leader. That fellow in the crumpled pajamas was Max the depleted, confused disciple.

My prayers were moans. My faith was a frazzled thread. I couldn't even summon the energy to fake it. I was honest. Honest to God, I was. Turns out God has a soft spot for an honest prayer.

Little by little I began to sense the Spirit. He led with a kind touch. He wooed with a whisper. Mysterious? By all means. But figment of my imagination? No. Not at all.

I requested strength. He gave it. I asked the Spirit to heal the sick. More than once he did. I prayed for vitality and joy. Both returned. The long winter thawed into a welcome spring.

One day while studying for a message, I read the words Jesus used to describe the Holy Spirit: *comforter* and *friend*. I recall having this wonderful realization: "I know that Person."

That was three decades ago. I no longer think of the Holy Spirit as the Holy Who. I now call him our Heaven-Sent Helper. He is the ally of the saint. He is our champion, our advocate, our guide. He comforts and directs us. He indwells, transforms, sustains, and will someday deliver us into our heavenly home.[2]

He is the executor of God's will on earth today, here to infuse us with strength. Supernatural strength.

Was this not the promise of Jesus? He would not let his followers begin their ministries unless they knew the Holy Spirit. "Don't begin telling others yet—stay here in the city until the Holy Spirit comes and fills you with power from heaven" (Luke 24:49 TLB).

By this point the disciples had spent three years in training. They had sat with him around campfires, walked with him through cities, witnessed him banish disease and command demons. They knew his favorite food, jokes, and hangouts. But they were not ready. They'd seen the empty tomb, touched his resurrected body, and spent forty days listening to the resurrected Christ teach about the kingdom. But they needed more.

"You shall receive power when the Holy Spirit has come upon you; and you shall be witnesses to Me in Jerusalem, and in all Judea and Samaria, and to the end of the earth" (Acts 1:8 NKJV).

Mark it down. The Holy Spirit comes with power. Power to make good choices, keep promises, and silence the inner voices of fear and failure. Power to get out of bed, get on with life, get busy about the right things in the right way. Power to face the unexpected, unwanted passages of time. Power. This is what Jesus promised then, and this is what Jesus promises still.

How is your power level?

Perhaps you have all the power you need. Life is a downhill stroll through a pleasant meadow. You never lack energy, enthusiasm, or strength. Your step has a spring to it; your voice has a song to it. You are ever the joyful, empowered person.

If that describes you, can I recommend a book on honesty?

If that doesn't describe you, consider the possibility of a life-giving relationship with the Holy Spirit.

No more walking this path alone. No more carrying weight you were not intended to bear. It's time for you to enjoy the presence of the Holy Spirit and experience the vigorous life he offers.

Your Bible makes more than a hundred references to the Holy Spirit. Jesus says more about the Spirit than he does about the church, marriage, finances, and the future. Why the emphasis on him? God does not want a bunch of stressed-out, worn-out, done-in, and washed-up children representing him in the world. He wants us to be fresher day by day, hour by hour.

But let's be careful. The topic of the Holy Spirit seems to bring out the extremists among us. On one hand there are the show-offs. These are the people who make us feel unspiritual by appearing super-spiritual. They are buddy-buddy with the Spirit, wear a backstage pass, and want everyone to see their healing gifts, hear their mystical tongue. They make a ministry out of making others feel less than godly. They like to show off.

On the opposite extreme is the Spirit Patrol. They clamp down on anything that seems out of line or out of control. They are self-deputized hall monitors of the supernatural. If an event can't be explained, they dismiss it.

Somewhere in between is the healthy saint. He has a child-like heart. She has a high regard for Scripture. He is open to fresh strength. She is discerning and careful. Both he and she seek to follow the Spirit. They clutch with both hands this final promise of Jesus: "You shall receive power when the Holy Spirit has come upon you" (Acts 1:8 NKJV).

God does not want a bunch of
stressed-out, worn-out, done-in,
and washed-up children
representing him in the world.
He wants us to be fresher day
by day, hour by hour.

Is it your desire to know the Holy Spirit better and to nurture your relationship with him? Then you and I are on the same page.

Scripture employs more than a dozen metaphors to describe the work of the Spirit. In fact, it is a testimony to his grandeur that one metaphor will not suffice.

Do you want to be wowed by Jesus? The Holy Spirit is the ultimate *teacher* (John 14:26).

Do you struggle to obey God's commands? The Spirit is the *wind* of God (John 3:8).

Do your prayers seem weak? He is our *intercessor* (Rom. 8:26).

Unsure of your salvation? He is the *seal of heaven* upon the saint (Eph. 1:13).

The Spirit is the *dove of peace* who calms us, the *gift giver* who equips us, the *river of living water* who flows out of us to refresh the world (Matt. 3:16; 1 Cor. 12:1–11; John 7:37–39).

The list goes on. Over the next few pages we will ponder the amazing benefit of the divine presence. Whether this is a fresh encounter or your first encounter, it does not matter. God wants you to have the energizing strength of the Holy Spirit.

Some time ago I was driving from one place to the next when I realized my gas tank was nearly empty. My indicator said I had less than ten miles worth of fuel. I spotted a convenience store and parked next to a pump. I placed the nozzle in my tank, swiped my card, and began filling up my car. I then set out to do all the things we do at such locations. I went into the store and bought a soda. I chatted with the store clerk. I thought about buying a hot dog but reflected on its contents and decided not to do so. I went back to my car and washed the windshield and emptied some trash out of my car. I removed the nozzle from the gas tank, climbed into my car, and was barely back on the road when I happened to look down at my gas gauge. It was on empty!

I'd like to say the pump clicked off prematurely. Knowing me and my attention span, however, I probably forgot to squeeze the lever.

The Spirit is the *dove of peace* who calms us, the *gift giver* who equips us, the *river of living water* who flows out of us to refresh the world.

I did everything except for the one thing I needed to do.

Does that describe your life? Have you forgotten the one thing you need to do? Have you neglected the Holy Spirit?

The Spirit of God longs to give you his great power. He will guide, teach, and energize you. He will shoulder the burdens you were never intended to carry.

Challenges come with life, but they need not define your life. Help is here.

CHAPTER 2

Come Alongside Me

The Spirit As a Teacher

*He will teach you all things, and bring to your
remembrance all things that I said to you.*
—JOHN 14:26 NKJV

I can't recall the fellow's name. Marco? Flavio? Luigi? It was an Italian name, for he was an Italian. He had that rugged Mediterranean look about him: dark hair, olive skin, and a handsome smile. He wore loose-fitting slacks, a silk shirt, and loafers. Pretty classy clothes. Then again, he was Italian.

He studied history in the university and made a living by leading tours through Rome. When our family had the opportunity to see the city, a friend of a friend of a friend gave us his name. He asked us what we wanted to see. Catacombs? Colosseum? Statues of Caesar?

Of course we wanted to see all of those. But the site at the top of my list, my *numero uno*, was the Sistine Chapel.

His eyes lit up. Do you know that classic Italian gesture of kissing the tips of the fingers as if something is of exquisite taste? He did it and said, "The Sistine Chapel. I will take you there."

He knew everything: the quickest route to the Vatican, the shortest lines in the Vatican, the names of the guards of the Vatican. He talked the entire time, all about the Sistine Chapel. The story of Michelangelo, the scaffolding, and the painting on the ceiling that forever changed the way we see Western art.

He walked fast, spoke faster. By the time we arrived, I wondered if the chapel would live up to its billing. It most certainly did. We craned our necks and looked up at the ceiling. After a few moments I glanced in his direction. He was smiling. He was thrilled that we were thrilled. He had this see-I-told-you expression on his face. For a few moments he said nothing. But then he scurried over next to me and in a whispered voice appropriate to the location pointed out details I would never have noticed without him. He walked me over to the corners to get a better view. He used Italian terms, but he was so enthused I didn't ask him to translate.

He changed the way I saw the chapel. I had admired it from afar. I had appreciated it from a distance. But on that day I was thrilled by it in person.

Wouldn't it be great if someone could do for the story of Jesus what this Italian did for the chapel?

If only we had an expert to teach us. Someone who knows Christ the way my friend knew the Sistine Chapel. Someone who can reveal him and remind us about him. Someone whose assignment is to stir in us a thrill about our Savior.

That Someone is alive and well. While I cannot recall the name of the fellow in Rome, Jesus made sure we all would learn the name of the Helper he left in charge. He called him the *Paraclete*. The word appears only five times in Scripture, and of those five times Jesus used it four, and he did so on the night before his crucifixion.[1]

> I will ask the Father, and he will give you another Helper [*Paraclete*], to be with you forever, even the Spirit of truth, whom the world cannot receive, because it neither sees him nor knows him. You know him, for he dwells with you and will be in you. . . .

The Helper [*Paraclete*] . . . whom the Father will send in my name, he will teach you all things and bring to your remembrance all that I have said to you. . . .

When the Helper [*Paraclete*] comes, whom I will send to you from the Father, the Spirit of truth, who proceeds from the Father, he will bear witness about me. . . .

It is to your advantage that I go away, for if I do not go away, the Helper [*Paraclete*] will not come to you. But if I go, I will send him to you. And when he comes, he will convict the world concerning sin and righteousness and judgment . . .

When the Spirit of truth comes, he will guide you into all the truth, for he will not speak on his own authority, but whatever he hears he will speak, and he will declare to you the things that are to come. He will glorify me, for he will take what is mine and declare it to you. (John 14:16–17, 26; 15:26; 16:7–8, 13–14)

So much in these passages deserves our attention.

Look at the unity of the Trinity. The Son will ask the Father, and the Father will send the Spirit. There is a happy cooperation at work here as if to say all of heaven sends help in the direction of the disciples of Jesus.

Also take note of the pronoun. Jesus doesn't want us to think of the Holy Spirit as an it or a thing. The Spirit is a person. And, like a person, the Spirit has intellect, emotions, and will. The Spirit speaks to the churches (Rev. 2:7), intercedes for the believer (Rom. 8:26), leads and commands the disciples (Acts 8:29; 16:6–7). The Spirit appoints elders (Acts 20:28), searches all things (1 Cor. 2:10), knows the mind of God (1 Cor. 2:11), and teaches the content of the gospel to us (1 Cor. 2:13). The Spirit dwells among and within believers (1 Cor. 3:16; Rom. 8:11; 2 Tim. 1:14), distributes spiritual gifts (1 Cor. 12:11), and gives life to those who believe (2 Cor. 3:6). He cries out from within our hearts (Gal. 4:6) and leads us in the ways of God (Gal. 5:18). He helps us in our weaknesses (Rom. 8:26), works all things together for our ultimate good (Rom. 8:28 THE MESSAGE), and strengthens believers (Eph. 3:16). He can be lied to (Acts 5:3–4), grieved (Eph. 4:30), insulted (Heb. 10:29), and blasphemed (Matt. 12:31–32).

This list would surprise most people. According to one study only four people in ten believe that the Spirit is a divine person. The rest of those surveyed either don't have an opinion or choose to believe the Spirit is more like a power surge than a divine being who empowers and teaches us.[2] That's regretful. How does one have a friendship with electricity?

Can you join me in a pledge? I hereby resolve never to call the Holy Spirit an it. The Spirit is a person. And Jesus calls him the *Paraclete*.

Translators land on different, yet similar, translations for this Greek word: "Comforter" (KJV), "Counselor" (ESV), "Advocate" (NEB), "Intercessor" (margin of the NASB). The Phillips translation interprets the name as "someone else to stand by you." The renderings may vary, but the central message is the same. We are not alone.

> The Spirit has a specific, overarching mission. His task is to teach us about Jesus.

Yet to what end? Is the Holy Spirit simply a divine companion who keeps us company? If so, that would be enough. Yet the Spirit has a specific, overarching mission. His task is to teach us about Jesus.

He will teach you all things and bring to your remembrance all that I have said to you. . . . When the Helper comes, whom I will send to you from the Father, the Spirit of truth, who proceeds from the Father, he will bear witness about me. . . . he will convict the world. . . . When the Spirit of truth comes, he will guide you into all the truth, for he will not speak on his own authority, but *whatever he hears he will speak, and he will declare to you the things that are to come.* He will glorify me, for he will take what is mine and *declare it to you.* (John 14:26; 15:26; 16:8, 13–14, emphasis mine)

Who would have imagined! The invisible presence of God on earth invites you to enter his classroom and learn from him.

The apostle Paul echoed this point in one of his letters. "No one's ever seen or heard anything like this, never so much as imagined anything quite like it—What God has arranged for those who love him. But you've seen and heard it because God by his Spirit has brought it all out into the open before you" (1 Cor. 2:9–10 THE MESSAGE).

Secularists look for answers in human philosophy and knowledge. The world religions look to the teachings of their now-dead founders: Muhammad, Buddha, Confucius. Christians, however, hold to this inscrutable and beautiful promise: our teacher not only spoke, but he speaks. He taught, yes, but he teaches still. His wisdom is not confined to an ancient document but is a part of the day-to-day curriculum of our mentor, the Holy Spirit.

As Paul goes on to say:

The Spirit, not content to flit around on the surface, dives into the depths of God, and brings out what God planned all along. . . . God offers a full report on the gifts of life and salvation that he is giving us. We don't have to rely on the world's guesses and opinions. We didn't learn this by reading books or going to school; we learned it from God, who taught us person-to-person through Jesus, and we're passing it on to you in the same firsthand, personal way. . . . Isaiah's question, "Is there anyone around who knows God's Spirit, anyone who knows what he is doing?" has been answered: Christ knows, and we have Christ's Spirit. (1 Cor. 2:10, 12–13, 16 THE MESSAGE)

We are not left alone with our questions. It is not up to us to solve the riddles of our existence. We have a helper, a divine instructor. He will save us from the cul-de-sac of confusion and the dead end of doubt. He does this by enrolling us in the primary course of his university: Jesus Christ. Look again at the Upper Room message:

> The Helper, the Holy Spirit, whom the Father will send in *my name*, he will teach you all things and bring to your remembrance *all that I have said to you*. . . . When the Helper comes, whom I will send to you from the Father, the Spirit of truth, who proceeds from the Father, *he will bear witness about me*. . . . .When the Spirit of truth comes, he will guide you into all the truth, for he will not speak on his own authority, but whatever he hears he will speak, and he will declare to you the things that are to come. *He will glorify me, for he will take what is mine and declare it to you*." (John 14:26; 15:26; 16:13–14, emphasis mine)

The chief aim of the Spirit is to escort you into the Sistine Chapel of Jesus and watch you grow wide-eyed and slack-jawed. He will enchant you with the manger, empower you with the cross, embolden you with the empty tomb. He will infect you with his love for the Savior.

He is downright bullish on Jesus.

J. I. Packer points this out beautifully, saying, "It is as if the Spirit stands behind us, throwing light over our shoulder, on Jesus, who stands facing us. The Spirit's message to us is never, 'Look at me; listen to me; come to me; get to know me,' but always, 'Look at *him*, and see his glory; listen to *him*, and hear his word; go to *him*, and have life; get to know *him*, and taste his gift of joy and peace.'"[3]

As Jesus foretold, "[The Spirit] will glorify me, for he will take what is mine and declare it to you" (John 16:14).

A classic example of this truth involves an encounter between two men: Peter, a devout Jew, and Cornelius, a God-fearing, God-seeking

We have a helper, a divine instructor. He will save us from the cul-de-sac of confusion and the dead end of doubt. He does this by enrolling us in the primary course of his university: Jesus Christ.

Gentile. They met several years after the ascension of Jesus. Their meeting was a complete surprise to Peter. Jews had nothing to do with Gentiles, especially those who served with the Roman army. Cornelius was an outsider. He didn't quote the Torah or descend from Abraham. Toga on his body and ham in his freezer. Uncircumcised, unkosher, unclean. Look at him.

Yet look at him again. He was kind and devout. "One who feared God with all his household, who gave alms generously to the people, and prayed to God always" (Acts 10:2 NKJV). Cornelius was even on a first-name basis with an angel. The angel told him to get in touch with Peter, who was staying thirty miles away in the seaside town of Joppa. Cornelius sent three messengers to fetch Peter. Peter, however, resisted.

But then "the Spirit said to him, 'Behold, three men are seeking you. Arise therefore, go down and go with them, doubting nothing; for I have sent them'" (Acts 10:19–20 NKJV).

The Spirit threw open the door of the gospel to welcome, not just the Jews, but the entire world.

Peter already knew that Jesus loved non-Jews. He had spent three years following Christ. Yet he needed a reminder. The Spirit gave it. "He will teach you all things, and bring to your remembrance [remind you] all things that I said to you" (John 14:26 NKJV). The phrase "bring to your remembrance" can mean "make contemporary."[4] The Spirit does more than repeat the words of Jesus; he makes them relevant. He unfolds their significance for the world in which we live.

I recall an afternoon early in my ministry when the invitation of Jesus to the weary became the invitation of Jesus to Max. I was supposed to be studying. But I could not concentrate. I was in the throes of the weariness I described in the last chapter, battling insomnia, a dozen insecurities, and deadlines. I was under the impression that I had to fix everyone's problems, shoulder everyone's burdens, and never grow weary in doing so. After some moments I moved from my office chair into the chair I used for guests. I bowed my head and sighed.

When I did, this scripture came to mind: "Come to Me, all who are weary and heavy-laden, and I will give you rest" (Matt. 11:28 NASB).

It was the pronoun *me* that got me. I had been turning to everyone and everything but him. The words of Jesus went from ink on a page to balm for my soul.

Why did that verse come to mind? Simple. The Holy Spirit, my teacher, reminded me. The Spirit of Christ will do this for you, my friend.

> And when the Spirit whispers in our ear . . . and makes us aware that Jesus is for real and his invitation is for real also, then he is fulfilling a further ministry, a *matchmaker* ministry, whereby he urges us, draws us, inclines us, moves us, to embrace the Lord Jesus, to say yes to his invitation, to go to him and make him, by faith, our own Savior, our own Lord, our own friend, our own king.[5]

Is this not great news! The Spirit, the Person present at creation, the one active in incarnation, the moving force in the resurrection, the mighty hand at the final revelation—he is your tutor. He will reveal new and wondrous things to you.

I came home the other day to find my wife, Denalyn, on the floor playing with our two grandchildren. She had purchased a half-dozen brightly colored, matchbox-sized cars. As I walked in, she was pulling them out of the bag. Rose and Max went crazy. That's what you'd expect of a four-year-old and a twenty-month-old toddler. Rose knew what to do. She recognized them as self-propelling cars. She took one and rolled it back and forth until the stored energy allowed the car to zip across the floor.

Max, on the other hand, had never seen them. The idea was new to him. Denalyn was thrilled to thrill him. She was on the tile floor, teaching Max how to roll the car back and forth until it was ready to be launched. When it exploded forward, oh how he laughed with glee. And when he laughed, Denalyn laughed twice as loud. She was so excited to see him excited.

The Paraclete wants to do the same with you. He will be a Denalyn to your world. The question is, Would you be a little Max to his? My grandson modeled the attitude we need—a childlike spirit. Hungry to be taught. Willing to be led. Humility is the soil out of which the fruit of the Spirit can grow.

> Humility is the soil out of which the fruit of the Spirit can grow.

Invite him into your world. Let your day begin with these words: "Welcome, Holy Spirit!" Make it your aim to walk in the Spirit by inviting him into the details of each day. "Since we live by the Spirit, let us keep in step with the Spirit" (Gal. 5:25 NIV). Let this prayer be quick to come to your mind: "In this moment what are you teaching me?" Or, "How am I to respond to this challenge, Lord?" Or, "Direct me, please. Which way should I go?" Pause and listen. Keep an ear inclined toward the Spirit.

I once participated in a golf outing that included caddies. It was amazing. My caddy not only carried my bag, he offered to tell me how to play. As we walked down the first fairway, he said, "I'll show you where to hit the ball and which club to use."

"How do you know?" I asked.

"I've been caddying here for twenty years."

I stopped, turned, and looked at him. "Twenty years? How many rounds of golf is that?"

He looked up at the sky as if he was calculating. "Around ten thousand."

Ten thousand! He knew each blade of grass by name. Every turn of the green and roll of the hill—he had experienced them. I asked, "Is there anything about this course you do not know?"

"Nope. I could play it in the dark."

So I peppered him with questions. How far should I hit this shot? He told me. Will this putt roll very fast? He told me. Should I quit golf and take up bowling? He told me. He told me because I asked him. For me not to consult him would have been foolish.

For us not to consult the Spirit of God would be the same. He is here to teach us. Our privilege is to stay in mindful communion with him. Day by day. Moment by moment.

Follow him into the Sistine Chapel of Jesus Christ. Listen as the divine instructor whispers wonders in your ear. Be assured that, as you smile, the Spirit smiles with you. After all, he is your teacher.

CHAPTER 3

Raise Your Sail

The Spirit As Wind

You send your Spirit, and new life is born to replenish all the living of the earth.
—Psalm 104:30 TLB

Not by might, nor by power, but by my Spirit, says the Lord of hosts.
—Zechariah 4:6

K atie Spotz and Laura Dekker have much in common. Both are endurance athletes. Both have boats. Both made headlines when they completed solo trips, Katie across the Atlantic, Laura around the world. Yet for all they have in common, there is this massive difference. One rowed; the other sailed.

Twenty-three-year-old Katie rowed, rowed, rowed her boat from West Africa to South America. Her 2,817-mile trip required seventy days, five hours, and twenty-two minutes. Her nineteen-foot yellow wooden craft was built to withstand hurricanes and fifty-foot waves. She was spared the hurricanes. The waves, however, kept her up at night. She packed half a million calories worth of freeze-dried meals, granola, and dried fruit. She rowed eight to ten hours a day and battled painful calluses.[1]

Laura Dekker, on the other hand, harnessed the power of the wind. In 2012 she became the youngest person to circumnavigate the globe solo. She used a two-mast, forty-foot sailboat named *Guppy*. The trip was not without its challenges. A court in the Netherlands, her native country, attempted to prevent it. Once at sea she had to sidestep reefs and survive numerous storms; her journey required one year and five months. But she made it.[2]

I do not plan to follow their examples. Endless days alone in the open water? I'd prefer a root canal with no pain killer. However, if forced to choose between rowing and sailing, I know my preference.

Do you know yours?

Spiritually speaking, which best describes your vessel? A rowboat or a sailboat?

The question is significant. We encounter stiff winds. Here is what God tells us to do:

> Care for the poor.
> Comfort the confused.
> Tell the truth.
> Forgive jerks.
> Pray constantly.
> Serve unselfishly.
> Pursue morality.

We are called to be . . .

> good stewards of money,
> good spouses to our mates,
> good members of society,
> good caretakers of the environment, and
> good employees in the workplace.

God challenges us to . . .

> find our gifts and use them,
> find the lost and reach them,
> find the prodigals and bless them,

find the confused and counsel them, and

control our tempers, lusts, greed, arrogance, tongues, laziness, appetites, and grumpy attitudes.

Are you tired yet? We'll sooner empty the ocean with a thimble than fulfill these assignments. Change the world? Why, most days we can't even change ourselves!

A friend tells about the day his ten-year-old son ran away from home. After being gone the entire day, the boy walked up the driveway with his head hung low. "Son," the father asked, "what did you learn today?" The boy answered, "I learned that everywhere I go, I take me with me."[3] Don't we all?

We take our greed, our selfishness, our wounds and warts. We dare not think for a moment that we have the power to be the person God wants us to be. But nor do we dare to think that God will fail to give it to us. He empowers us to be what he calls us to be. This was the promise Jesus made to a certain religious leader who paid him a late-night visit.

"Now there was a man of the Pharisees named Nicodemus, a ruler of the Jews" (John 3:1). There were only six thousand Pharisees in Israel. Nicodemus was numbered among them. There were only seventy-one clerics on the high counsel; he was one of them. Jesus even called him "the teacher of Israel" (v. 10), implying a special status. Nicodemus was as religious as a Southern Baptist Convention.

"This man came to Jesus by night and said to him, 'Rabbi, we know that you are a teacher come from God, for no one can do these signs that you do unless God is with him' " (v. 2).

He was careful and tactful. Careful to come at night, lest he be spotted conversing with the upstart rabbi. Tactful to flatter, lest he fail to make a good first impression. Jesus, however, was not careful nor tactful. He was forceful. Though Nicodemus asked no question, Jesus gave him an answer. "Jesus answered him, 'Truly, truly, I say to you, unless one is born again he cannot see the kingdom of God'" (v. 3).

Keep in mind, Jesus was talking to a bishop of sorts. If religion were an academic enterprise, Nicodemus would have had a wall full of diplomas. Jesus was unimpressed with his credentials. He told Nicodemus, "You must be born again," as if to say, "Go back to the beginning and start over."

A bit radical for someone as finely frocked as Nicodemus. The Pharisee was taken aback. He questioned, "How can a man be born when he is old? He cannot enter a second time into his mother's womb and be born, can he?" (v. 4 NASB).

Nicodemus spoke only four sentences in this brief conversation. In those four sentences he used the word *can* four times:

"No one can . . ." (v. 2)

"How can . . ." (v. 4)

"Can he . . ." (v. 4)

His final question will appear in verse 9 with yet another: "How can these things be?"

Nicodemus was obsessed with what a person can and cannot do. He was all about human effort, human gumption, human achievement. In his view the gate to heaven was greased with elbow grease.

Jesus, to the contrary, made four references to human *in*ability. Absent the help of heaven, we . . .

1. cannot see (i.e., experience) the kingdom of God (v. 3),
2. cannot enter the kingdom of God (v. 5),
3. cannot give birth to the Spirit (v. 6), and
4. cannot discern the movements of the Spirit (v. 8).

This is a classic conversation. On one side Nicodemus, representing all well-meaning, God-fearing, Bible-toting, law-abiding, tax-paying, tithe-giving, candle-lighting, pew-sitting, scripture-memorizing, boat-rowing folk. On the other, Jesus Christ.

And what the latter says to the former is so un*can*ny that it sends shock waves through church pews and synagogues to this very day. "I assure you, no one can enter the Kingdom of God without being born of water and the Spirit. Humans can reproduce only human life, but the Holy Spirit gives birth to spiritual life" (3:5–6 NLT).

The phrase "Kingdom of God" refers to a relationship with God in this life and entrance into heaven in the next. This is high stakes! How do we receive citizenship? Be born again.

In our first birth we become brand-new humans. In our second birth we become brand-new creations. And who oversees our second birth? The Holy Spirit![4] Indeed, were it not for the work of the Spirit, the new birth would be impossible! "No one can say, 'Jesus is Lord,' except by the Holy Spirit" (1 Cor. 12:3 NIV).

If Nicodemus was having trouble keeping up with Jesus' comments, we can hardly fault him. He'd barely said, "Good evening," and Jesus, in rapid fire, told him about a new kingdom, a new birth, and the power to experience them both. But Jesus was just getting warmed up.

"The wind blows where it wishes, and you hear its sound, but you do not know where it comes from or where it goes. So it is with everyone who is born of the Spirit" (John 3:8). When it came to describing the Holy Spirit, Jesus had a universe of metaphors at his disposal. Comets. Galaxies. Ocean depths. Beluga whales. And out of the entire glossary, he chose this word picture to give to Nicodemus: wind. It's easy to see why.

The Spirit, like wind, is an unseen force.

Dutch theologian Abraham Kuyper dedicated years and more than a thousand pages to the study of the Holy Spirit. The first chapter of his book is entitled "Careful Treatment Required" and contains this paragraph:

Of Him nothing appears in visible form; He never steps out from the intangible void. Hovering, undefined, incomprehensible, He remains a mystery. He is as the wind! We hear its sound, but can not tell whence it cometh and whither it goeth. Eye can not see Him, ear can not hear Him, much less the hand handle Him.[5]

The Spirit is wholly holy and unlike any being in our world.

Which is such good news! We need alien assistance, a source of strength that is unbuffeted by that which buffets us, undisturbed by that which disturbs us, untethered to whatever ties us down. The Spirit is not subject to weather patterns, aging bodies, pandemics, stock market swings, or despots. He has never been sick. He will never be afraid. He does not worry, strive, or struggle. He is the Holy Spirit, marked by mystery and characterized by majesty.

"The wind blows where it wishes . . ." (v. 8).

In like manner the Holy Spirit answers to no government or organization. He does not report to a president, priest, prince, or pastor. He blows where he wishes. Mighty enough to clear a path. He can break down walls of prejudice and subdue the most stubborn heart. Yet gentle. So soft as to barely rustle a leaf. A roaring wind at Pentecost. A still, small voice at Mount Horeb.

The Spirit is like the wind. Had Jesus stopped with this comment, Nicodemus would have had plenty to ponder. Yet Jesus went on to stretch the imagination of Nick and Max and all people who have tried to quarry the jewels that follow.

"So it is with everyone who is born of the Spirit" (v. 8).

That which is born of a vegetable is a vegetable. That which is born of a dog is a dog. That which is born of a fish is a fish. And that which is born of the Spirit is Spirit. That is to say, we have his wind, his unseen power, within us. We host the mystery and majesty of God.

What we cannot do, he can. Stop and think about something you struggle to do. What uphill climb is taking your breath? Forgiving an enemy? Solving a problem? Breaking a habit? You can't do it? The Spirit can. You have the force of heaven's wind within you.

I consider myself to be a bit of an expert on the force of wind. I was raised in windy country. Springtime winds average twelve miles per hour in my hometown. (There is an oft-told joke about a West Texas rancher who returned from a trip to New York City with a swollen nose. He was so accustomed to leaning into the wind that when there wasn't one, he kept falling on his face.)

Some enterprising entrepreneur thought a buck could be made off this wind. He set up a sailboat-for-rent business on the shore of the city lake. The sailboats were the length of a surfboard with a single mast and sail. My friend James and I were among the first customers. Neither of us knew how to sail, mind you. West Texas generates wind, not sailors.

We climbed aboard and shoved off. Or did we shove off, then climb aboard? Either way we floated out onto the lake and for a few delightful moments enjoyed life on the high seas. But then our momentum ceased. I looked at James, and James looked at me, and we shrugged. We had no clue how to untie the mast or hoist the sail. So we did the only thing we knew to do. We jumped into the water, positioned ourselves behind the boat, and got to work.

The image of two clueless teens kicking their way to the dock might serve as a picture of many well-intentioned Christians. We spend every drop of energy self-propelling our way to shore.

Jesus invites us to hoist the sail.

Row-boat Christianity exhausts and frustrates. Those who attempt it are left depleted and desperate at the attempt. Those who let the Spirit do the work, on the other hand, find a fresh power. Life still has storms. The water grows rough. But they are not left to face the fury on their own.

Nicodemus was fixated on the word *can*. The Christian is fixated on the word *done*. The work of salvation is done. God helps those who admit they cannot help themselves.

Does that describe you? Can I urge you, if you have not done so already, to believe on him whom God has sent. Trust Jesus to do the work that only he can do. Rely upon the Holy Spirit to quicken within you a new spirit, a new creation. No more ceremony. No more huffing and puffing. Gone is the endless list of dos and don'ts and the deadening thought that having done much, you haven't done enough. No more coming to Christ in the dark of the night in fear.

Come to him in the light of a new day! In the power of a new you.

A few nights ago our neighborhood experienced a power outage. Not a power shortage, mind you, but a power outage. Electricity was cut off. The line between the generator and the residences was severed. There was no electricity. None. Nada. Zilch. Zero. Had a meter reader come to our house, he would have seen no activity on the gauge.

Lamps, dark. TV, dark. The AC went off. The microwave did not work. The refrigerator was on its way to becoming an oven. The ceiling fans went still. Denalyn and I, from one instant to the next, went from a room alit with lights to a dark, silent cave.

Fortunately we knew exactly what to do. Younger, less experienced individuals might have been bewildered, befuddled, or afraid. Not the missus and me. We've been around long enough to know how to react. We sprang into action.

Denalyn oversaw the ceiling fans. She grabbed a ladder and, with the aid of a flashlight, began to spin the blades. She rotated the fan as ferociously as she could. "Are you feeling the air?" she asked me between huffs and puffs.

"Not yet, sweetheart. Keep it up. You'll ventilate the house soon." I needed her to succeed. I was working up quite a sweat with the light switch. Thinking I could generate power with activity, I flipped the switches on and off, on and off, on and off. No luck, but I was not discouraged.

I stood in front of the TV and set in motion mission number two: activate with screaming. "Come on! Get after it! Do your job. We want to see some color, hear some voices, watch some programs."

The lack of response only deepened my resolve. I realized I could flip the switches and yell at the TV simultaneously. So I scurried back to the switch, bumping my shin on the coffee table in the process, and re-engaged my wrist and resumed my screams.

All in all the room was abuzz with activity.

Denalyn spinning the fan.

Max flipping the switch.

Max yelling at the TV.

When power did not return, we stayed at it. Oh, you should have seen us. You would have been so impressed.

What's that? Unimpressed? From which side of the truck did we fall? Say that again. Frenzy is no source of energy?

I'm so glad to hear you say those words. That was the message of Jesus to Nicodemus. That is the message of Jesus to us. We cannot fulfill our mission on our own. We do not have the strength, resolve, or power. But the Spirit does. So trust him. Hoist the sail, take a breath, and enjoy the ride.

CHAPTER 4

Groans of the Heart

The Spirit As Intercessor

*God's Spirit is . . . making prayer out of our
wordless sighs, our aching groans.*
—ROMANS 8:26 THE MESSAGE

*Even now my witness is in heaven;
my advocate is on high.
My intercessor is my friend
as my eyes pour out tears to God;
on behalf of a man he pleads with God
as one pleads for a friend.*
—JOB 16:19–21 NIV

A microscopic virus has shut us down. As I write these words, COVID-19 has crippled the economy, parlayed global anxiety, and killed multitudes of people. It's a tsunami of fear. When I began writing this book, phrases like "shelter in place," "social distancing," and "flatten the curve" were unheard of. Now they are common lingo. Masks cover our faces, fear shrouds our hearts, and the dread of a fatal inhale has shut our doors.

By the time you read these words, I pray this pandemic has passed. If it has, let this observation be included in the history books: we did not know how to pray.

I know this to be true because I created a virtual prayer page. Each day I posted an online message of hope and this open invitation: "Post your prayers and we will pray for you." The page was flooded with requests. From Connecticut to Cambodia they came. Hundreds of thousands of statements like these:

"Pray that I find some work."
"Pray that I get along with my family."

"Ask God to help me sleep."

"I'm lonely. Pray for someone to call me."

But the most common request was the most heartfelt one.

"I don't know what to ask. Just pray for me."

"I'm at a loss for words. Can you mention my name?"

"I try to pray but can't. Most of the time I just weep."

"I'd pray, but the needs are too great for words."

"All I can do is sigh."

The groans of the heart. You have heard them. You have made them. They are the vernacular of pain, the chosen tongue of despair. When there are no words, these are the words. When prayers won't come, these will have to do. Sunnier days hear nice, poetic petitions, but stormy seasons generate mournful sounds of sadness, fear, and dread.

Yet these raw appeals find their way into the presence of God the Father. How can we be sure? Because they are entrusted into the care of the Holy Spirit.

We know that the whole creation has been groaning as in the pains of childbirth right up to the present time. Not only so, but we ourselves, who have the firstfruits of the Spirit, groan inwardly as we wait eagerly for our adoption to sonship, the redemption of our bodies. . . . The Spirit helps us in our weakness. We do not know what we ought to pray for, but the Spirit himself intercedes for us through wordless groans. And he who searches our hearts knows the mind of the Spirit, because the Spirit intercedes for God's people in accordance with the will of God. (Rom. 8:22–23, 26–27 NIV)

Few passages reveal the tender heart of the Holy Spirit as much as this one. We're accustomed to his mighty deeds. Fire falling on Peter. Doors opening for Paul. Because of the Spirit, Ezekiel saw dead bones rise, and Moses saw the Red Sea open. Yet of equal import is this: the Spirit curates and translates the incoherent prayers of the weak until they are heard in the tribunal of heaven.

We, "who have the firstfruits of the Spirit, groan inwardly" (v. 23). The presence of the Spirit does not guarantee the absence of pain. Pain is a part of every life. This pain leads to a feeling of weakness. Paul's chosen term for "weakness" appears in other places in his epistles in reference to physical affliction. He mentions his own affliction (Gal. 4:13), as well as the illness of Timothy (1 Tim. 5:23). Infirmity, it seems, was in the forefront of Paul's mind.

Sickness saps our energy. I recall a bout with atrial fibrillation that left me battling a rapid heartbeat for months on end. The condition drained my strength and grayed my sky. Doctors were baffled, and I was discouraged. I would slip into our sanctuary and kneel at a prayer altar and offer unadorned petitions.

My weakness was nothing compared to some of yours. When cancer robs the vigor of youth. When multiple sclerosis siphons the breath of life. When rheumatoid arthritis stiffens our joints. In these times our prayers become groans.

Perhaps your weakness emerges from a different source. You're weak from a crumbling marriage. Weak from a business failure. Weak from the rejection of a loved one. Weak from unemployment. It is in such times that the mind is too troubled to articulate a prayer. We are like Hezekiah, who confessed:

> I moan like a dove.
>
> My eyes are weary with looking upward. (Isa. 38:14)

Or the psalmist who wrote:

> I am feeble and utterly crushed;
>   I groan in anguish of heart.
> All my longings lie open before you, Lord;
>   my sighing is not hidden from you. (Ps. 38:8–9 NIV)

There is often a gap between what we want from life and what we get in life. And during such times of weakness "we do not know what to pray for as we ought" (Rom. 8:26).

Thank you, Paul, for this honest admission. If you, the apostle and author of most of the Epistles, did not always know how to formulate a prayer, we take heart, for there are times we do not either.

What should the cancer patient request? Healing or deliverance into heaven?

For what should the father of the prodigal pray? God's patience for his son? Or a pigpen for his son?

For what should the persecuted prisoner ask? Release from captivity? Or endurance in captivity?

We do not know how to pray as we ought. What if our prayers are too sparse to deserve an audience with God? What if he turns us away? Others pray with boldness, resolve, and assurance. We read of prayers that opened prison doors for Peter and healed the sick for Paul. Yet we can barely utter an "Our Father." Does heaven hear the enfeebled prayers of a weary soul?

Thanks to our heavenly helper the answer is yes. "The Spirit himself intercedes for us" (v. 26 NIV).

To intercede is simply to stand in between. When a strong person takes up the cause of a weak one, intercession happens.

My wife and I experienced an intercession in 1983. When Denalyn and I moved to Rio de Janeiro, Brazil, we were the greenest of gringos. We scarcely spoke Portuguese. We'd never lived outside of the country. We'd read books on cross-cultural adaptation, but no book can prepare you for the moment you step off the plane without a return ticket.

Our adjustment was particularly challenging because our possessions were stuck in Customs. We had a crate full of furniture, family pictures, dishes, books, pots, and pans, but we could not get to them. Our apartment was empty. The crate was full. All we needed was the Customs official to release it to us.

For several weeks I made regular trips to the Customs office. In my broken Portuguese I asked the official if my crate could be released. "No, Senhor." His explanation included words like *delayed, needs approval, return tomorrow*. I didn't understand the problem, nor did I understand the language sufficiently to make my case. We were at an impasse.

Imagine the dread I felt as I returned day after day to tell Denalyn, "I can't get it out."

Enter Quenho, our next-door neighbor. Literally he and his wife entered our apartment and introduced themselves to us. We had no place for them to sit, so we stood as we sipped our coffee. I explained my plight.

Quenho began to smile. "I'll help you," he said. "I'm a lawyer."

I told him I'd already tried for a month.

He was nonplussed. "I can do this."

Could he ever. We walked into the Customs office, and Quenho approached the same official who had rebuffed me time and time again. Within moments the two men were laughing. Quenho pointed at me and motioned for me to step over. He put his arm around my shoulder and said something to the official about being my neighbor. There may have been an exchange of some money. I'm not sure. All I know is that it worked. The crate was released. Our furniture was delivered, and my wife was very, very happy.

Quenho had everything I did not. He understood the culture.

He knew the language. He could interpret the law. He perceived the problem. He knew how to persuade the Customs official. And, fortunately for us, he chose to speak on our behalf.

He was our advocate.

This is the role of the Holy Spirit. In those moments when you have nothing going for you, be assured, you have God's Spirit as your advocate. "Even if people can do no more than sigh for redemption, and then fall dumb even as they sigh, God's Spirit already sighs within them and intercedes for them."[1]

> In those moments when you have nothing going for you, be assured, you have God's Spirit as your advocate.

We do not know how to pray as we ought, but the Spirit does. And does he ever! Unlike the Customs official, your Father is more than willing to release blessings in abundance. You have the Spirit as your advocate and your Father as your provider. You may feel weak, but you've never been stronger.

As a result the greatest prayer warriors might very well appear to be the weakest ones: the convicted criminal in jail, the immigrant at the border, the forgotten child in the orphanage. The prayer shawl of depression is every bit as holy as the one made of linen. My mother, riddled with dementia, would lie in her bed and mumble. Our good God heard her. When the veteran with PTSD longs for the courage to reenter society, is this not a heaven-worthy prayer?

Right now, at this moment, as I write these words and you read them, the Spirit of the living God is talking to the rest of the Trinity about you. The eternal, unending, ever-creating Spirit is speaking on your behalf. He . . .

[is] making prayer out of our wordless sighs, our aching groans.
(Rom. 8:26 THE MESSAGE)

intercedes for us with groanings too deep for words. (ESV)

pleads with God for us in groans that words cannot express. (GNT)

Do you not find this amazing? Help is here! The greatest force, the only true force, in the universe is your ally, your spokesperson, your advocate. "[He] keeps us present before God. That's why we can be so sure that every detail in our lives of love for God is worked into something good" (v. 28 THE MESSAGE).

What you pray in the night is heard in the light of your Father's throne. "You keep track of all my sorrows. You have collected all my tears in your bottle. You have recorded each one in your book" (Ps. 56:8 NLT).

Let this assurance add value to your time of prayer. The apostle Paul did. If he were asked, "How is a person to walk in the Spirit?" he would say, "Pray!" His life was devoted to prayer. He prayed regularly and continuously and urged us to do the same (1 Thess. 5:16–18). "On all occasions," he urged, "pray in the Spirit" (Eph. 6:18 NIV).

On a June day in 2018, twelve boys made a decision that nearly cost them their lives. They descended into the recesses of the Tham Luang cave in Thailand. The plan was simple: poke around for about an hour, emerge with fun memories, and then cycle home. That was it.

No one expected the water.

A sudden storm flooded the passageways, trapping the group inside. They had no food and no light, utter darkness, and no communication with the outside world. The cave was deep, and they were irretrievably trapped.

The boys had no way of knowing, but people around the world were praying for them. We did not know how to pray, but even so, we prayed. God heard our prayers. A network of nations developed a rescue operation. The effort involved more than ten thousand people—divers, rescue workers, soldiers, helicopter pilots, ambulance drivers—as well as diving cylinders, sniffer dogs, drones, and robots. A world of know-how and can-do was brought to bear on their behalf.

It took the workers nine days, but divers eventually found the boys huddled on a muddy ledge. The rescuer removed his mask and told the boys, "I'm just the first. Others are coming."[2]

Can you imagine how they felt when they heard those words? If so, you can imagine how the Spirit wants you to feel as he says, "What you cannot say, I will say. Do not despair. Your prayers are being heard in heaven."

You aren't trapped beneath a kilometer of earth. But you may be stuck in a dark place with no visible exit. If so, please hear this. When we are in times of weakness, it is all hands on deck as the Trinity works to bring about what is good for us. We do not know how to pray. That is okay. The Holy Spirit knows. And he prays for you.

CHAPTER 5

A Sure Salvation

The Spirit As a Seal

For I am convinced that neither death nor life, neither angels nor demons, neither the present nor the future, nor any powers, neither height nor depth, nor anything else in all creation, will be able to separate us from the love of God that is in Christ Jesus our Lord.
—ROMANS 8:38–39 NIV

I shall lose none of all those he has given me.
—JOHN 6:39 NIV

P erhaps you can relate to this tender childhood memory. My parents and grandparents conspired for me to spend a week under the care of my grandmother and grandfather. I may have been ten years old, if that. I was just a lad. The plan was simple: Mom and Dad would drive me to the bus station, buy me a ticket, and see me off on the three-hour trek. My grandparents would drive to the bus station closest to their house, await my arrival, and take me to their home. My job, as recited multiple times by my mother, was to plant myself in the seat and not get off at any of the stops along the way. If I did get off, it was to be only for reasons of biological necessity. "Do your business, talk to no one, and get back on board." If Mom said it once, she said it a dozen times.

She had reason to be worried, of course. The road can be a treacherous place. Kids get lost. Kids get snatched. Kids get rebellious. Despite the danger, my parents took me to the bus station.

As I was about to step onto the bus, my dad did a reassuring thing. He took a small amount of cash, paired it with a prewritten note, and stuck both in my shirt pocket. "Buy yourself some candy." He gave me a hug. Mom gave me a kiss. Off I went.

As per my instructions I stayed put and watched the West Texas cotton fields blur past. We stopped at thriving towns like Seminole, Slaton, and Idalou, but I didn't exit. Only when I spotted my grandma did I climb down from the bus. The trip went off without a hitch.

Indeed, the only reason it deserves to be mentioned is because of the note Dad stuck in my shirt pocket. Just a few miles into the trip I retrieved the money and the slip of paper. "This boy belongs to Jack and Thelma Lucado," it read. The note contained our home address and phone number. In the unlikely event that I was separated from the bus, this message, he hoped, would reconnect me to my family.

It brings me great joy to say this: God did the same with you. Look into the shirt pocket of your spirit, and you will see it. He laid public claim to you: "This child is mine." You and I need the protection. The road can be a treacherous place. His kids get lost. His sons and daughters grow rebellious. The evil one can lure us. God wants Satan and Satan's minions to know, "This one belongs to me. Keep your hands off."

To whom does the Trinity entrust your protection? You "were sealed with the promised Holy Spirit" (Eph. 1:13). Later in the same epistle Paul urges us "not [to] grieve the Holy Spirit of God, by whom you were sealed for the day of redemption" (Eph. 4:30). In both passages the apostle spoke in simple past tense so as to emphasize an accomplished deed. We are not *being sealed*, nor do we *hope to be sealed*. We have been *once-and-for-all-time sealed* by the Spirit for redemption.[1]

Seal. You know the verb. You twist a jar lid to seal the pickles. You lick an envelope to seal the letter. You notarize the contract to seal the deal. Sealing declares ownership and secures contents. Sealing is the act that says, "This is mine, and this is protected."

When you accepted Christ, God sealed you with the Spirit. He cocooned you, assuring your safekeeping. Satan might woo you, discourage you, and, for a time, influence you. But he cannot have you. Christ "has identified you as his own, guaranteeing that you will be saved on the day of redemption" (Eph. 4:30 NLT).

When it comes to divine imprimatur, you and Jesus enjoy the same status. He said, "God the Father has set His seal on [Me]" (John 6:27 NKJV). The Greek word used to describe both the seal of Jesus and the seal of the saint is identical.[2] Would Jesus fear rejection from his Father? By no means. Should you fear the same? No!

Not only are you sealed, *you are adopted.*

> For all who are led by the Spirit of God are children of God.
>
> So you have not received a spirit that makes you fearful slaves. Instead, you received God's Spirit when he adopted you as his own children. Now we call him, "Abba, Father." For his Spirit joins with our spirit to affirm that we are God's children. And since we are his children, we are his heirs. (Rom. 8:14–17 NLT)

You are no slave. The slave lives in fear, fear that the master won't approve of work done, fear that the master will not provide for the future. What is to keep the master from selling the slave at any point?

The father-child relationship, however, is one of assurance.

In the Old Testament, God is described as a father only fifteen times. In the New Testament he is referred to as our father more than two hundred times. The New Testament is much smaller than the Old Testament. So what happened between the Old and New?[3]

Christ happened. His death on the cross was the final payment for our sins. "As far as the east is from the west, so far has he removed our transgressions from us" (Ps. 103:12 NIV). How far is the east from the west? Farther and farther by the moment. Travel west and you'll never go east. Journey toward the east and you'll never go west. Not so with the other two directions. If you travel north or south, you'll eventually reach the North or South Pole and change directions. But east and west have no turning points.

Neither does God. His forgiveness is irreversible.

"You will tread our sins underfoot and hurl all our iniquities into the depths of the sea" (Mic. 7:19 NIV). The Hebrew word used for "hurl" sounds like "shaw-lak."⁴ God gives our sin a good shellacking. He hurls our sins into the deepest ocean. He doesn't stockpile them in a room or shove them beneath a carpet; he catapults them into the sky and lets them splash and sink into the distant waters, never to be recovered or used against us. He has fully dealt with them. Your sins are submerged at sea, loaded on the eastbound train while you fly toward the sunset.

> Headline this truth: when God sees you, he does not see your sin.

Headline this truth: when God sees you, he does not see your sin. God "blots out your transgressions" and "remembers your sins no more" (Isa. 43:25 NIV). No probation. No exception. No reversals. God will not change his mind about you.

You are adopted by God. This idea is amazing in any era. Yet to the audience of the apostle Paul, it was especially significant. By Roman law an adopted son . . .

- lost all relationship to his old family. Everything was gone, and he gained all rights to the new family,
- became heir to the father's estate,
- was forgiven of all prior debts,
- and was, in the eyes of the law, the son of his new father.⁵

This is what Christ made possible for us. We are undeniably God's. Our past might as well have never happened. We have nothing to do with our old identity. The Holy Spirit convinces us of this transaction.

He "joins with our spirit to affirm that we are God's children" (Rom. 8:16 NLT).

> You can tell for sure that you are now fully adopted as his own children because God sent the Spirit of his Son into our lives crying out, "Papa! Father!" Doesn't that privilege of intimate conversation with God make it plain that you are not a slave, but a child? And if you are a child, you're also an heir, with complete access to the inheritance. (Gal. 4:6–7 THE MESSAGE)

The natural attitude of people toward God is not like this. We might repeat the phrase "Our Father in heaven," but we do not mean it. We do not really trust him, love him, or pursue him. Apart from the work of the Spirit, we see God as a deity to avoid, appease, or even escape. We dread God. If we come to him in prayer, it is out of duty or fear and not love.

But upon conversion a supernatural change occurs. Our affection toward God begins to warm. We turn to him. We trust him. We begin to perceive him as the perfect Father. We can do this "because the love of God has been poured out within our hearts through the Holy Spirit who was given to us" (Rom. 5:5 NASB).

The Spirit convinces your spirit of this truth: your destiny is in the hands of a loving Father. Your name is not written in God's book with a pencil. He does not hover an eraser above your entry, just waiting for an excuse to remove it. He is no cruel master who demands perfection and promises retribution. He is a good Father, who has recorded your name in the Book of Life with the blood of the Lamb. And the Spirit of God is urging you to listen as he affirms in your spirit that you are a child of God. You have been adopted into the family. "God affirms us, making us a sure thing in Christ, putting his Yes within us. By his Spirit he has stamped us with his eternal pledge—a sure beginning of what he is destined to complete" (2 Cor. 1:21–22 THE MESSAGE).

Your name is not written in God's book with a pencil. He does not hover an eraser above your entry, just waiting for an excuse to remove it. He is no cruel master who demands perfection and promises retribution. He is a good Father, who has recorded your name in the Book of Life with the blood of the Lamb.

Some time ago I heard a dear friend describe the day she became a Christian as the most wonderful day of her life. She said the next day was the worst day of her life. I asked why.

She explained, "I awoke with the thought 'What if I mess it up?'"

Can you relate? Do you fear your faith might fail?

Robert Harkness was a gifted Australian pianist who traveled the world in his twenties with the famous evangelist R. A. Torrey. One night at an evangelistic rally in Canada, Harkness met a young man, recently converted, who feared he might not be able to stay saved. Harkness longed for the young man and others like him to have confidence in God's ability to keep them, to know that he finishes what he starts.

Harkness mentioned the need in a letter to London hymn writer Ada Habershon. Inspired, she wrote the song "When I Fear My Faith Will Fail."

> *When I fear my faith will fail, Christ will hold me fast*
> *When the tempter would prevail, He will hold me fast*
> *I could never keep my hold through life's fearful path*
> *For my love is often cold, He must hold me fast.*
> *He will hold me fast, He will hold me fast*
> *For my Savior loves me so, He will hold me fast.*
> *Those He saves are His delight, Christ will hold me fast*
> *Precious in His holy sight, He will hold me fast*
> *He'll not let my soul be lost, His promises shall last*
> *Bought by Him at such a cost, He will hold me fast.*[6]

Why is this security important? Why does this matter? Why do you need to know that you are adopted by the Father and sealed by the Spirit? Simple. There is power in assurance.

A young college graduate requested that I pray for her to be accepted into law school. She filled out the forms and made the submission and waited . . . and waited. Each time we talked, she seemed increasingly anxious. *What if I don't get in? What will I do in the next semester? Have I selected the wrong profession?*

The unknown future unsettled her.

But then came the acceptance letter. "We are pleased to inform you . . ."

She called me with the great news. Her voice was strong and thoughts were positive. She immediately kicked into a higher gear. She was planning to find an apartment, review the curriculum, shop for some new clothes. Why the change in her outlook? She knew what was coming next. Her future was secure.

The Holy Spirit provides a far more significant assurance. From him we receive an acceptance letter, not to law school, but to heaven.

> So we will not be afraid on the day of judgment, but we can face him with confidence because we live like Jesus here in this world.
>
> Such love has no fear, because perfect love expels all fear. If we are afraid, it is for fear of punishment, and this shows that we have not fully experienced his perfect love. We love each other because he loved us first. (1 John 4:17–19 NLT)

Are you a Christian who fears judgment? Let the prayer of Robert Robinson be yours:

> *Prone to wander, Lord, I feel it,*
> *Prone to leave the God I love;*
> *Here's my heart, O take and seal it,*
> *Seal it for Thy courts above.*[7]

God loves you with a perfect love: perfect knowledge of your past mistakes, perfect knowledge of your future missteps, and, yet, is perfectly willing to love you despite both. He is committed to getting you home safely.

Nic Brown understands the value of such assurance. He was the first person in his county to be diagnosed with the coronavirus. He was thirty-eight years old at the time, a healthy father of two daughters. As a resident of a rural county in Ohio, he has no idea how he contracted the disease.

But he did. The disease attacked with a vengeance. As his health declined, he was transferred to the intensive care unit of the Cleveland Clinic and placed on full life support. His condition so deteriorated that the hospital had end-of-life discussions with his wife. His medical team monitored his treatment by writing goals for each day on the glass door of his room. At the end of the notes, they would leave this special message of resolve: "We will get you home."

Little by little Nic's body began to combat the virus. The recovery was gradual, yet complete. Nic was eventually reunited with his daughters and his wife. The caretakers had kept their promise.[8]

The Holy Spirit will keep his. We've been sealed. He will get us home.

CHAPTER 6

Calm This Chaos

The Spirit As a Dove

*I am leaving you with a gift—peace of mind and
heart! And the peace I give isn't fragile like the peace
the world gives. So don't be troubled or afraid.*
—JOHN 14:27 TLB

Svalbard, Norway, the safest place on Earth. At least that's what the Global Seed Vault is banking on. They're the brains behind an ultrahigh security and ultralow temperature bank vault that has the capacity to house seeds of every plant we eat, more than 4.5 million of them.

Even if Svalbard isn't the safest place on Earth, it's certainly one of the coldest and farthest north. Below-zero-degree weather is common. Polar bears outnumber humans. The frigid temperature and sparse population uniquely qualify it to safeguard agriculture against catastrophe. Underground concrete bunkers are built to withstand floods, fires, and nuclear attacks. In the event of global warming or worldwide plague, the seeds are safe.

Most of us can't hide out in a bunker. Yet the threats of calamity might make us try to do so. If the global temperature rises a few more degrees . . . If classified information falls into sinister hands . . . If the wrong person pushes the wrong red button . . . It's enough to make a person purchase a flight to Svalbard.[1]

And as if the worldwide perils weren't enough, we face personal ones. Blood cell count goes up. Savings account goes down. Marriage goes south. Pandemics rage. Work goes off the rails. Stress goes off the charts. Can't sleep. Can't eat. You are powerless to calm this inner storm.

The result? Anxiety. The emotion is not a sign of weakness, immaturity, or demon possession. It is simply the result of living in a fast-changing, challenging world. Anxiety is not a sign of weakness. But anxiety does weaken us. It takes our sleep. It numbs our minds. It clutters our hearts with dread. Yet help is here. You have at your disposal the surest antidote for trepidation. The Holy Spirit. He is the calming presence of God in the world today. He will help you defy the voices of fear and draw nigh to the presence of peace.

His first act in earthly history was to turn chaos into calm. "The earth was without form, and void; and darkness was on the face of the deep. And the Spirit of God was hovering over the face of the waters" (Gen. 1:2 NKJV).

The earliest depiction of our planet is not a welcoming one. My imagination conjures up images of spewing lava, random comets, colliding waves, and lightless corridors. There was no life, light, or pleasant sound—only chaos, abyss, and seething pandemonium.

Yet in that moment of primal frenzy, we see the inaugural appearance of the Holy Spirit: "hovering over the face of the waters."

We might expect a different verb. The Spirit of God *ruled, commanded, directed,* or *declared.* Yet the inaugural activity of the Holy Spirit was to hover over a frenzied world. This word *hovering* appears rarely. In one of the other occasions, it is used again in the context of chaos. God's relationship to ancient Israel is described as a hovering, protective eagle.

> As an eagle stirs up its nest,
> Hovers over its young,
> Spreading out its wings, taking them up,
> Carrying them on its wings. (Deut. 32:11 NKJV)

Can you envision the squawking eaglets, mouths open, heads bobbing? The nest is a swarm of energy, inexperience, and inability. But here comes momma eagle. Her presence calms her flock. Her provision nourishes her eaglets. Her task is simple: calm the chaos.

In like manner the Spirit of God hovered over the face of the waters. And once there was calming, there could be creating.

> The earth was without form, and void; and darkness was on the face of the deep. And the Spirit of God was hovering over the face of the waters. *Then* God said, "Let there be light"; and there was light. (Gen. 1:2–3 NKJV, emphasis mine)

Before God created the world, the Spirit of God calmed the world.

The Old Testament begins with a description of the Spirit as a hovering, settling presence. How fitting then that early in the New Testament we see a story of the Spirit as a gentle dove.

> Then Jesus came from Galilee to John at the Jordan to be baptized by him. And John tried to prevent Him, saying, "I need to be baptized by You, and are You coming to me?"
>
> But Jesus answered and said to him, "Permit it to be so now, for thus it is fitting for us to fulfill all righteousness." Then he allowed Him.
>
> When He had been baptized, Jesus came up immediately from the water; and behold, the heavens were opened to Him, and He saw the Spirit of God descending like a dove and alighting upon Him. (Matt. 3:13–16 NKJV)

John the Baptist did his best to talk Jesus out of the baptism, seeking to reverse the roles. But Jesus would have none of it. And so it was that the two men waded into the cobalt-colored waters, felt the mud between their toes, and smiled at the crowd that stood on the bank of the river. John got Jesus good and wet, and as Jesus was coming out of the water, the heavens opened, and the Spirit, like a dove, descended on him.

All four Gospels tell of this moment (Mark 1:10; Luke 3:22; John 1:32). Luke in his Gospel goes so far as to say the Spirit descended, not like a dove, but as a dove. "The Holy Spirit in the form of a dove settled upon him" (Luke 3:22 TLB). The Holy Spirit is depicted in many different forms in Scripture: a fire, a wind, oil in a lamp, and a river surging with living liquid. But here at the coronation of Christ, the Spirit chose to descend gently, softly, kindly, as a dove.

Would a hawk not have been more apt? Ever ready to pounce on Satan, the rat? Or an owl, the symbol of wisdom? Perhaps a meadowlark, serenading the world with music? Yet the Spirit chose to come as a dove. Why?

Part of the answer might lie in the maternal tenderness of the Holy Spirit. In biblical times the dove was a feminine symbol, and the Hebrew word for Spirit was feminine.[2] "Doves are commonly considered a symbol of motherhood because of their unique ability to produce their own milk. . . . They cease foraging for food just before their babies are born. This temporary starvation ensures a purer milk formulation for their offspring."[3]

The Holy Spirit, like a mother, ministers to us with affection.

I could always tell when my daughters came home in a troubled mood. Their first question would be "Where is Mom?" Her response to their troubles was different from mine. I would enter fix-it mode. I reacted with strategies and solutions. Denalyn, however, reacted with warmth and empathy. She would listen. She would hold her daughter. She would let her talk as long as she wanted to talk. She was sympathetic.

There are occasions when we need a father's strength, and God, our Father, provides it. There are occasions when we need the friendship of a brother, and Jesus, our spiritual sibling, offers it. Yet there are many times in which our spirits are troubled and anxious. We long for the tranquil assurance of a loving mother. For this we turn to the Holy Spirit.

The Holy Dove of God soothes the noisy, tumultuous, excitable, and vindictive atmosphere of the human heart. "The fruit of the Spirit is . . . kindness . . . gentleness" (Gal. 5:22–23 NKJV).

Could you use some of the same? A 2018 study by the American Psychiatric Association revealed that 51 percent of Americans describe themselves as anxious, tipping the scales in favor of worry for the first time.[4]

Satan peddles this fear. I'm convinced he runs a school dedicated to one topic: the Language of Anxiety. Somewhere in the bowels of hell, classrooms of demons are taught the dialect of dread and doubt. Were you to sit in on this class (not recommended), you would see the professor of advanced panic stalking about the room, parlaying the fine art of fear distribution. He points his bony finger in the air and speaks through a snarl. "You must sow seeds of distress in the minds of these children of God."

"Exaggerate, overstate, and amplify," he says. "Wake them up in the middle of the night. Better still, keep them awake so they cannot rest. Make sure they assume the worst. Urge them to envision a world of no escape, no solution, and no hope."

Were you to eavesdrop on a class (again, not recommended), you would hear his mousy minions rehearsing the declarations of trepidation.

No one will ever help me!

It's all over!

Everyone is against me!

I'll never get through this!

The demons graduate with one assignment: to stir faith-robbing, nail-biting, sleep-stealing unease.

Are they whispering in your ear?

Our stress-laden society has developed many skills for dealing with anxiety. We have breathing exercises and meditation techniques. We have medications and seminars. These tools have their place. But the person in whom the Spirit dwells has the greatest of resources. Turn to him for help. The next time a wave of anxiety begins to roll over you, go immediately to the Spirit in worship.

The apostle Paul said:

> Do not get drunk on wine, which leads to debauchery. Instead, be filled with the Spirit, speaking to one another with psalms, hymns, and songs from the Spirit. Sing and make music from your heart to the Lord, always giving thanks to God the Father for everything, in the name of our Lord Jesus Christ. (Eph. 5:18–20 NIV)

The apostle contrasts two strategies for facing inner chaos: inebriation and celebration. Many people numb themselves, if not with liquor, with long weeks of work, bouts of shopping, or hours of playing. Anyone who has tried this approach knows its falsehood. Happy hours do not make us happy. We may forget our troubles for a moment, but they are awaiting us as we leave the bar.

> The next time a wave of anxiety begins to roll over you, go immediately to the Spirit in worship.

The better option? Celebration. Fill the air with "psalms, hymns, and spiritual songs" (NCV). Paul used a verb tense that caused one translation to state: "ever be filled and stimulated with the [Holy] Spirit."[5] Constant worship clears the debris from our hearts. Praise is the cleansing element that flushes the trash of worry and anxiety.

Paul and Silas modeled this practice. Enemies had dragged them before the magistrates of the Roman outpost of Philippi. Authorities

Constant worship

clears the debris

from our hearts.

Praise is the

cleansing element

that flushes the trash

of worry and anxiety.

beat them with rods. These rods tore the skin, raised welts, caused bruising, and perhaps broke ribs. Soldiers then imprisoned them in the deepest part of the prison where it was damp, cold, and rat infested. To increase security and misery, their feet were put in stocks (Acts 16:24).

There they lay all afternoon and into the night, in foreign territory, with no local advocates, their backs open to infection, surrounded by darkness, shivering from cold, unable to adjust their position, hundreds of miles from home. What was their response?

> Along about midnight, Paul and Silas were at prayer and singing a robust hymn to God. The other prisoners couldn't believe their ears. Then, without warning, a huge earthquake! The jailhouse tottered, every door flew open, all the prisoners were loose. (Acts 16:25–26 THE MESSAGE)

Oh, to have heard that midnight song. They sang so heartily that the other prisoners heard them.

Paul and Silas did not know how this story would end. They had not read Acts 16. They were not sure of their deliverance. But they were sure of their deliverer. You can be too.

Rather than panic, you can choose to praise.

Those devils and their whispering lies? Stand against them. Those voices with their seeds of doubt and defeat? Silence them. You outrank Lucifer and his hordes. Your example is that of Jesus Christ.

When the storm came into his world, what did he do? "He . . . rebuked the wind, and said to the sea, 'Peace, be still!' And the wind ceased and there was a great calm" (Mark 4:39 NKJV).

When the demon took charge of a man in the synagogue, how did Jesus respond? "Jesus rebuked him, saying, 'Be quiet, and come out of him!'" (Mark 1:25 NKJV).

Do likewise. The Holy Spirit will give you the power; you just have to use it. When the storm of fear comes, speak against it. When the evil one draws near, rebuke him! Stand firm against the forces of hell. "For God has not given us a spirit of fear, but of power and of love and of a sound mind" (2 Tim. 1:7 NKJV).

Let me show you how this works. It's midnight. You've been trying to get to sleep since ten o'clock, but you cannot. You have a big meeting tomorrow. You need some rest. You try the different sleep-inducing strategies: slow breaths, counting sheep, listening to a Lucado sermon, but nothing works. Your mind won't shut off.

You begin to envision worst-case scenarios. You will forget your notes. You'll call your boss by the wrong name. Your thoughts spin around in descending circles, taking you down, down, down until you are in a pit. You pound your pillow, and your heart pounds in your chest. The old version of you might have spent the night staring into the dark. But a new version of you is taking shape. A version that has received the fullness of the Holy Spirit. A version that does not face challenges alone but turns quickly to worship.

So here is what happens. You climb out of bed and find a quiet place where you can open your Bible and pray. You read the verses that promise peace from the Holy Spirit.

> GOD met me more than halfway,
> he freed me from my anxious fears. . . .
> When I was desperate, I called out,
> and GOD got me out of a tight spot.
> GOD's angel sets up a circle
> of protection around us while we pray. (Ps. 34:4–7 THE MESSAGE)

You select a favorite song, either to listen to or to sing. Maybe both. If one isn't enough, you sing some more. Then you pray. You pray in the Spirit, and the Spirit prays in you. You surrender tomorrow to the care of your loving God. And then, to make sure the devil knows he has failed, you tell him to leave you alone. *I belong to Jesus Christ, thank you very much. So you must depart from here.*

Indeed, he must. And he will.

Will you fall fast asleep? Probably. But if not, stay at it.

The Holy Spirit will do for you what my daughter did for her son. It was a big day for little Max. His first haircut. Everyone was excited. Everyone, that is, except Max. His sixteen months of life had yet to prepare him for this moment. It did not matter that he got to sit in a miniature fire truck. It did not matter that he was promised a piece of candy. He was undistracted by the cartoons on the TV. All he saw was a woman he did not know coming at him with a pair of scissors.

He began to cry. His daddy tried to comfort him. His grandma did the same. I told him he would someday wish he had hair to cut. Made no difference. But then came Mama. She leaned down and whispered in his ear words that the rest of us could not hear. He still was unhappy, but he calmed down enough to complete the event.

The Spirit, the mother heart of God, will soothe you as well. He calmed the creation. He descended as a dove. Take a deep breath and relax. The Spirit of God is here to help.

CHAPTER 7

How to Hear from God

The Spirit As a Pillar of Cloud and of Fire

*In your great mercy you didn't abandon [the Israelites] to die
in the wilderness! The pillar of cloud led them forward day by
day, and the pillar of fire showed them the way through the night.
You sent your good Spirit to instruct them, and you did not
stop giving them bread from heaven or water for their thirst.*
—NEHEMIAH 9:19–20 TLB

*I will put my Spirit in you and move you to follow
my decrees and be careful to keep my laws.*
—EZEKIEL 36:27 NIV

A friend of mine is all about the Game of Life. He loves it. Much to his chagrin I'd never heard about it. He gave me a what-planet-are-you-from look and began describing what he believes is the perfect board game.

Here's the gist. The board contains a pathway through life and a series of squares. There is a set of cards, cars, a spinner, some tokens, a few people pegs, a few mountains, buildings, and a bridge or two. Upon the prompting of a spinner, the players advance a certain number of squares. The square invites them to make a choice. (Or did the card invite them to move forward a square?) Either way they make a fork-in-the-road decision. Career or college? Borrow money or make a purchase?

"Eat a burger or spaghetti?" I chuckled. My friend didn't smile. "It's all about the decisions we make and the consequences that follow," he explained. "Buy it and try it out. It is manufactured by—"

I interrupted him. "No need to tell me. I know the inventor."

"You do?"

"Yes. I spoke to him just this morning."

"You spoke to the creator of Life?"

"I did. I spoke to him when I prayed."

My friend still didn't think I was funny. But I was correct.

According to God's plan life is a series of decisions. Do I move or stay? Hold on or let go? Tie the knot or not?

Small decisions. Large decisions. Decisions everywhere! We make our choices, and they make us. Consequently, decision-making saps energy and creates anxiety. What if I make the wrong choice? What if I go south when I should go north?

So what can we do? Given the weightiness of choices, how can we make good ones? You will be encouraged by the promise of Scripture. We can be led by the Holy Spirit: "He leads me in paths of righteousness for his name's sake" (Ps. 23:3).

God, our Good Shepherd, doesn't just feed us; he leads us. He does more than correct us; he directs us. He keeps us on track. He has commissioned the Holy Spirit to guide us down the winding roads of life.

A vivid example of this promise is found in the saga of the Hebrew people.

They had spent a lifetime within the confines of the small nation of Egypt. They'd never crossed the border. Then, in a furiously fast turn of events, Pharaoh set them free. Centuries of slavery were behind them; a new future was ahead of them. The Red Sea opened, and the promised land beckoned. It was theirs for the taking. Yet they were rookie sojourners. They'd never left their city limits. On their own they stood no chance of survival. For that reason,

The LORD went ahead of them in a pillar of cloud to guide them on their way and by night in a pillar of fire. (Ex. 13:21 NIV)

The pillar of cloud also moved from in front and stood behind them, coming between the armies of Egypt and Israel. (Ex. 14:19–20 NIV)

In all the travels of the Israelites, whenever the cloud lifted from above the tabernacle, they would set out; but if the cloud did not lift, they did not set out—until the day it lifted. (Ex. 40:36–37 NIV)

Can you imagine the blessing of this divine GPS? On any given day God told them where to go. To the east is a valley, to the west an open plain. Straight ahead is a series of rolling hills. Which direction is the right one? Moses and the leaders pause until the massive cloud turns. Once it does, they follow. The stress of decision-making was reduced to keeping an open eye toward heaven.

We can thank Isaiah the prophet for telling us the name of the force within the cloud and fire.

> Where is he who set
>   his Holy Spirit among them,
> who sent his glorious arm of power
>   to be at Moses' right hand,
> who divided the waters before them,
>   to gain for himself everlasting renown,
> who led them through the depths?
> Like a horse in open country,
>   they did not stumble;
> like cattle that go down to the plain,
>   they were given rest by the Spirit of the LORD.
> This is how you guided your people
>   to make for yourself a glorious name. (Isa. 63:11–14 NIV)

Who led the ex-slaves through the Red Sea and through the wilderness? The Holy Spirit.

Who leads the children of God today? The Holy Spirit! We have what the Hebrews had minus the manna.

Jesus gave this assurance: "When he, the Spirit of truth, comes, he will guide you into all the truth" (John 16:13 NIV).

Yet how can we learn to follow him? Why do we at times fail to detect him? How can we be led by the Spirit?

Here is a direct answer:

Don't copy the behavior and customs of this world, but let God transform you into a new person by changing the way you think. *Then you will learn to know God's will for you,* which is good and pleasing and perfect. (Rom. 12:2 NLT, emphasis mine)

God has a will for you that is "good and pleasing and perfect." To know it, you must not "copy the behavior and customs of this world." His voice must outrank the voices of society. God wants us to be different. Not odd. Not peculiar. Our aim is not to blend in but to look up.

God would later tell the Hebrew people, "Do not follow the crowd in doing wrong" (Ex. 23:2 NIV).

Following the crowd can lead a person off the cliff. Just ask the Turkish shepherds who watched nearly 1,500 sheep do exactly that. For some undetermined reason a single sheep jumped over the edge. The first was followed by a second, then a dozen, then several dozen. Pandemonium ensued. There was nothing the shepherds could do. Nearly 1,500 animals jumped, and 450 died.[1] The others would have perished as well, except that they landed on the bodies of the first jumpers.

Those sheep weren't thinking. If they were, they were saying to themselves, "Well, the jumpers look dumb. But a few hundred sheep can't be wrong, right?" Yes, they can. So can people. Don't copy the behavior and customs of this world. You cannot hear the Spirit if you are listening to them. You can't soar like an eagle if you are running with dumb sheep.

Don't copy the behavior
and customs of this
world. You cannot hear
the Spirit if you are
listening to them. You
can't soar like an eagle
if you are running with
dumb sheep.

If you want to hear from God, the first question you need to ask is not "What should I do?" but "Whom will I hear? Who has authority? Who calls the shots in my life?" If the answer is "people," you will not discern God's direction. If the answer is television personalities, you will not discern God's will for your life. Add to that list horoscopes, palm readers, and tarot cards. If you are following the stars, you aren't following the Son. "The true children of God are those who let God's Spirit lead them" (Rom. 8:14 NCV).

Stop following a culture that doesn't follow God and . . .

Start listening for the Spirit, who speaks on behalf of God.

During the wilderness wanderings there came a wonderful moment. The position of the fiery and cloudy pillars changed. God had instructed Moses to build a tabernacle in which he would dwell. Once the project was complete, the majestic cloud, which had hovered above them, descended from on high and entered the holy place. "Then the cloud covered the tabernacle of meeting, and the glory of the LORD filled the tabernacle" (Ex. 40:34 NKJV). The presence of God stooped from the skies and settled between the cherubim on the mercy seat of the ark of the covenant. From then on, God was not at a distance. He was among his people.

My imagination conjures up the sight of the cloud and fire intertwining and then descending like a cyclone, ever spinning until the motion stopped directly over the tabernacle. From that moment on every child of Israel could point to the tabernacle and say, "God is in there."

With that image in mind, I ask you to gesture to your heart and say, "God is in here." On the day you decided to follow Jesus, an unseen miracle occurred. The Holy Spirit descended from the heavens, like a cyclone maybe, ever spinning until the moment the motion stopped directly over your body. He took up residence within you. You became his dwelling place.

This was the promise of Jesus: "The Spirit of truth . . . lives with you and will be in you. . . . Anyone who loves me will obey my teaching. My Father will love them, and we will come to them and make our home with them" (John 14:17, 23 NIV).

He turned your heart into his tabernacle. "Don't you know that you yourselves are God's temple and that God's Spirit dwells in your midst?" (1 Cor. 3:16 NIV).

The Spirit of God dwells within you. The Spirit moves within us to lead us. He does so with two tools: the verse and the voice.

"Take the helmet of salvation and the sword of the Spirit, which is the word of God" (Eph. 6:17 NIV). The primary communication tool of the Holy Spirit is the Bible. He speaks to us through Scripture. His will is found in his Word. "Your word is a lamp to guide my feet and a light for my path" (Ps. 119:105 NLT).

The crowd says: Your value depends on your net worth.

Scripture says: You matter because God made you (Eph. 2:8–10).

The crowd says: Do what you want. It won't hurt.

The Bible says: "There is a way that seems right to a man, but its end is the way to death" (Prov. 14:12).

The crowd says: If there is a God, he does not care about us.

Scripture says: "For God so loved the world, that he gave his only Son" (John 3:16).

Scripture has an answer for any issue you face. The Bible is not only inspirational but also extremely practical.

> The primary communication tool of the Holy Spirit is the Bible. He speaks to us through Scripture.

I have an example from my days in South America. We missionaries did not know if we were supposed to pay income tax to the government of Brazil. Our income was from the US, thereby technically untaxable. However, we were living in Brazil, using services and roads. Should we not pay tax? When I looked to see if the Bible had anything to say about this peculiar and unique-to-me question, I found the most interesting story. On one occasion Jesus told Peter that, as Jews, they weren't really obligated to pay taxes to the Romans.

> "But we don't want to upset these tax collectors. So go to the lake and fish. After you catch the first fish, open its mouth and you will find a coin. Take that coin and give it to the tax collectors for you and me." (Matt. 17:27 NCV)

Who would have imagined? The Spirit of God used the Word of God to give me an answer to my question. So I went fishing! Just kidding. I already had the coin; I just needed to know if I should give it. He will give guidance to you as well. Go first to the verse.

Go next to the voice.

The voice might be your inner sense, the "knowing" that results from Scripture interacting with the Spirit. The voice might be wise counsel, a dream, or a vision.

There was an occasion in which the apostle Paul and his companions attempted to enter a city, "but the Spirit did not permit them" (Acts 16:7 NKJV). Soon thereafter "a vision appeared to Paul in the night. A man of Macedonia stood and pleaded with him, saying, 'Come over to Macedonia and help us'" (v. 9 NKJV). Paul obeyed. A woman named Lydia was baptized, and Europe had its first convert.

There was an occasion in which the leaders of the church in Antioch were seeking God's will. "They were all worshiping the Lord and fasting for a certain time. During this time the Holy Spirit said to them, 'Set apart for me Barnabas and Saul to do a special work for which I have chosen them.' So after they fasted and prayed, they laid their hands on Barnabas and Saul and sent them out" (Acts 13:2–3 NCV).

In what manner did they hear the voice of the Spirit? I do not know. Was the voice an audible one? I do not know. Did the Spirit speak through one leader to the others? I do not know. Did the clouds in the sky form in the shape of letters and spell a word? I don't know.

What I do know is this: The Spirit spoke. He still does.

So talk to him. Ask him to guide you. Seek his will. And then listen. Wait for a response. As we follow him, we begin to discern his voice. I've noticed that he often speaks to me through my own thoughts. This is not surprising. He owns my mind. My body is his temple. I should not be surprised that his answer to my question would come in a form that I can understand.

The phrase "led by the Spirit of God" is such a happy one. The Spirit does not drive us like cowboys drive cattle. He gently leads us as a shepherd would lead a flock of sheep. Scripture refers to God as our Shepherd more than two hundred times! He is more committed to leading us than we are to following him. So relax! If you don't sense his guidance, ask again.

"Trust in the LORD with all you heart, and lean not on your own understanding" (Prov. 3:5 NKJV). He is completely capable to lead you where he wants you to go.

He might use a nudge, a prick of the conscience, a reminder of Scripture. The Spirit speaks first through the verse. He may complement the verse with a voice. Then again, the verse may be enough.

Don't make the mistake the fellow made with the bakery. He told his wife that he was going to discontinue his daily stop for donuts. She was surprised when he came home later that day with a freshly baked dozen.

"I thought you weren't going to stop at the bakery."

"I wasn't," he explained. "But as I drove past it, I felt the nudge to go in. I prayed, *Lord, should I buy some donuts? I will circle the bakery. If I am supposed to buy donuts, let there be an open parking place.*

"Well, honey," he continued. "There was an open place. I had to circle the bakery ten times, but I found an open parking place."

Don't manipulate circumstances until they say what you want to hear.

Go first to the verse. His will never contradicts his Word. Are you seeking direction? Open your Bible. Are you in need of guidance? Open your Bible. Are you at a crossroads in life? Open your Bible. When you open your Bible, God opens his mouth.

The verse and the voice. The Spirit uses both to lead us to the promised land. God is calling. Keep listening. He created the game of life and is happy to show us the way to play it.

CHAPTER 8

Soul on Fire

The Spirit As a Flame

*I baptize you with water, but one who is more
powerful than I is coming. . . . He will baptize
you with the Holy Spirit and fire.*
—LUKE 3:16 NRSV

B rad Haugh still remembers the sound of his heartbeat. It thundered in his chest. Two hundred beats a minute. With a fire behind him and a ridge ahead of him, this smoke jumper needed every pulse of power his heart could give in order to escape with his life.

He was one of forty-nine firefighters caught in a wildfire on the spine of Storm King Mountain, seven miles west of Glenwood Springs, Colorado. Fourteen of them lost their lives. They were overrun by flames that Haugh estimated to reach a height of three hundred feet. The wall of heat required only two minutes to race a quarter of a mile up the mountain, reaching a speed of eighteen miles per hour. Temperatures reached two thousand degrees, hot enough to incinerate the tools dropped in its path.

"People were yelling into their radios, 'Run! Run! Run!' I was roughly one hundred and fifty feet from the top of the hill, and the fire got there in ten or twelve seconds. I made it over the top and just tumbled and rolled down the other side, and when I turned around, there was just this incredible wall of flame."[1]

Few of us will ever find ourselves trying to outrun a fire. But all of us have had encounters with fire. We've extended cold hands over the warm campfire. We've lifted a burning torch into the dark night. We've ignited the blue flame of the gas stove and beheld the red glow of hot metal. Fire is a part of life. For that reason when fire and the Holy Spirit appear in the same sentence, we take note.

"He will baptize you with the Holy Spirit and fire" (Matt. 3:11). This is how John the Baptist introduced his cousin to the world. We might have expected a more, can we say, positive outlook. "He will baptize you in happy feelings." "He will lift your self-image so you will feel good about yourself." "He will make it easier for you to have friends and deal with conflict." But baptize you with the Holy Spirit and fire? Such was the job description of Jesus.

The words echo the prophecy of the Old Testament's final book.

> For He is like a refiner's fire
> And like launderers' soap.
> He will sit as a refiner and a purifier of silver;
> He will purify the sons of Levi,
> And purge them as gold and silver,
> That they may offer to the LORD
> An offering in righteousness. (Mal. 3:2–3 NKJV)

Heaven arrives packing heat. And this heat, we shall see, is good for the heart.

Please note that Jesus is the giver of the Holy Spirit fire. "He will baptize you." The Greek language emphasizes the exclusive role with "he himself" (*autos*). Do you desire the Spirit? Then turn to Christ. Receive him as Savior and Lord. He, then, will "baptize" you in the Spirit. He will plunge, immerse, and submerge you in the very being of the Spirit. Just as Jesus stepped out of the river dripping the Jordan, so we step forth into the world drenched in the Spirit of heaven. Nary a hair on our heads is left out of the process. Every part of us, top to bottom, is designed to be blessed by the Holy Spirit and with fire.

The soul baptized in the Spirit is a soul ablaze.

> The soul baptized in the Spirit is a soul ablaze.

Fire is a chemical reaction that releases energy in the form of light and heat. In the case of a wood fire, the energy was originally derived from the sun and stored in the plant as cellulose and lignin. Heat from another fire or a lightning strike converts the cellulose into flammable gases, which are driven out of the wood and combined with oxygen. If there is enough air, fuel, and heat, the fire will keep advancing.

Can't something similar be said about the Spirit of God? If we let him do his work, he will not be set back. He will not be put out. He will not be quenched.

Yet this flame is never intended for our harm. Quite the contrary. Everything that is good about a fire can be listed as a blessing of the Holy Spirit.

Fire is a purifying force. My mom, a nurse, taught us this principle when we were very young. She used a needle on our skin to remove a thorn or lance a sore. She did so after she had twirled the sharp tip in the hot flame of a match. "I want to kill the germs," she explained. Fire does this. It purifies.

The Holy Spirit is the ultimate purifier. He comes to eradicate the defilement from the vessel. Are we fit to serve as a temple of the Holy Spirit? We need the cleansing, sanctifying work of heaven to prepare us for this assignment. So the Spirit comes not just to purify but to beautify, not just to cleanse but to adorn.

This refining fire is not always pleasant. It can come in the form of discipline or disappointment, setback or loss. Yet the fire of the Spirit produces ultimate good. Do we not see this in nature? The American Forest Foundation lists several benefits of forest fires. They . . .

- release seeds or otherwise encourage the growth of certain tree species, like lodgepole pines;
- clear dead trees, leaves, and competing vegetation from the forest floor so new plants can grow;
- break down and return nutrients to the soil;
- remove weak or disease-ridden trees, leaving more space and nutrients for stronger trees;
- keep tree stands thin and open, letting more sunlight in so trees stay healthier; and
- improve wildlife habitat.[2]

A fire, managed and contained, results in ultimate good for the vegetation. When Jesus baptizes us in the fire of the Spirit, it is so we can bear better and more abundant fruit for him.

Welcome this refining fire. Invite him to finish this work in your heart. "Though outwardly we are wasting away, yet inwardly we are being renewed day by day" (2 Cor. 4:16 NIV). In the next life your heart will have been refined of all dross. Jealousy, gone. Greed, gone. Guilt, gone. Regrets, anxiety, and pride, gone forever. This time on earth is a time of preparation, and God's person of preparation is the Spirit. Let him do his work in you.

Don't do with your soul what I used to do with my shirts. My first position out of seminary was a pastoral internship in St. Louis, Missouri. I shared an apartment with two other single fellows. Our housekeeping skills left much to be desired. We were expected to wear a coat and tie when representing the church and the internship. I owned one sports coat and a couple of dress shirts. They suffered from overuse. My budget was too tight for dry cleaning, so I learned to launder and iron the shirts myself. One of my roommates noticed how long it took me to iron a shirt and showed me his trick. Only iron the visible parts. Under his tutelage I mastered the art of pressing my shirt collar and cuffs. Had anyone asked me to remove my coat, they would have seen a shirt that was as wrinkled as a wadded-up sheet of paper.

The Spirit of Jesus won't fall for this foil. He wants access to every square inch of our souls. There is nothing that is hidden from him. Make this a part of your daily prayer: "God, examine me and know my heart; test me and know my anxious thoughts. See if there is any bad thing in me. Lead me on the road to everlasting life" (Ps. 139:23–24 NCV).

The Spirit, like a hot iron, can straighten out the crumpled areas of your life so you'll feel no need to hide them.

He will give you power over the struggle of sin. Many Christians can relate to these words of the apostle Paul: "Wretched man that I am! Who will deliver me from this body of death?" (Rom. 7:24).

This sobering confession is the exclamation point on the apostle's remembrance of his life before he followed Christ. Each day was a day of defeat. Many people feel the same way. They assume that the temptations of today are here to stay and that life is a head-forward battle against the headwinds of failure and fear.

If that is you, observe what Paul says just a few verses later. Romans 8 is Paul's great statement of liberation. In contrast to the previous chapter, he speaks of victory and assurance and grace. The difference? Chapter 7 was life under the old law (v. 9). Chapter 8 is life in the Spirit. In chapter 7 the pronoun "I" occurs twenty-seven times, and the Holy Spirit is mentioned once. In the eighth chapter the pronoun "I" appears only twice, and references to the Holy Spirit appear twenty-two times.[3] The point? Victory over sin is the result of the presence of God's Spirit within us.

The Spirit, like a hot

iron, can straighten

out the crumpled areas

of your life so you'll feel

no need to hide them.

Which chapter reads more like your life? Are you dependent upon "I"? Or "him"? "Do not put out the Spirit's fire" (1 Thess. 5:19 isv). Don't quench his fire by dismissing his presence or resisting his leading.

Fire melts away the frozen, cold ice of winter. The fire of the Spirit does the same. Without the Holy Spirit we tend to harden. We need his presence to thaw out our resistant hearts. As he shines his light, you can expect to love people whom you used to resist. Those old biases and racist attitudes? They will not long stand beneath the heat of he who loves all humanity. You, like the Spirit, will feel a burden for lost people of other countries, untaught people of other languages. You will have greater compassion and kindness, all because the Spirit shed forth a warmth through you.

Perhaps the greatest characteristic of fire is this: energy. It is the secret of the electric current. It has empowered countless coal-burning engines and fueled too many stoves to count. Fire combusts. Fire ignites. Fire moves things.

And the Spirit? Does he not move us? "You shall receive power," promised Jesus, "when the Holy Spirit has come upon you" (Acts 1:8 NKJV).

God doesn't want us just to give him our best effort. He wants us to look to him as the source of our effort. We don't try our hardest and then turn to God. We turn to God and trust him to do the work for and in us. We "can do everything through Christ, who gives [us] strength" (Phil. 4:13 NLT).

The greatest force in the universe will work within you to give you the power you need to become more and more like him. He will make you holy, in an instant, and he will make you holier over a lifetime.

When the fire within seems to flicker, what can we do? One of the most practical answers has to do with the importance of the church.

In her book about the Holy Spirit, Anne Graham Lotz tells about a young man who returned from college and stopped in for a visit with his pastor. The two entered the cozy study of the minister and chatted about the boy's life at college, his new friends, and classes. The pastor asked the student if he'd found a church to attend. "No sir," the young man answered, "I don't feel the need to go to church anymore. My faith is strong enough without it, and with my studies and activities I just can't find the time."

The pastor said nothing but reached over, pulled a log from the fire, and left it on the hearth. He leaned back in his chair, folded his hands, and remained silent. After several moments the student assumed the pastor had dozed off. He stood to leave.

"Did you think I had fallen asleep?" asked the older gentleman. "I was just watching that log I pulled out of the fire. Did you notice? When it was in the fire with the other logs, it burned brightly. But now that I've removed it, the fire has gone out. Son, you are like that log. If you expect your faith to stay on fire, you need to be in fellowship with other believers."[4]

The church is far from perfect. Even so, the church is the campfire God uses to keep us kindled. "Let us consider how to provoke one another to love and good deeds, not neglecting to meet together, as is the habit of some, but encouraging one another, and all the more as you see the Day approaching" (Heb. 10:24–25 NRSV).

There is one final attribute of fire that reminds us of the Holy Spirit. Fire is a protective element. The eastern shepherd would surround his fold at night with a wall of fire, keeping the wild beasts out and the sheep safe within. So God says, "I myself will be a wall of fire around it . . . and I will be its glory within" (Zech. 2:5 NIV).

The fire of the Spirit deflects a thousand temptations. He loves you too much to leave you unguarded. The evil one can see you, but he cannot reach you. He may bare his fangs, but he will not set them into your skin. The Spirit is the artillery around you, defying the demons and their tricks.

Welcome his help. He will purify, refine, energize, and protect. No one can do more than he.

CHAPTER 9

Oily Footprints

The Spirit As Anointing Oil

God anointed Jesus of Nazareth with the Holy Spirit and power.
—ACTS 10:38 NIV

God's love has been poured out into our
hearts through the Holy Spirit.
—ROMANS 5:5 NIV

I came home to the most delightful fragrance the other day. "Honey, what's that smell?" The aroma stopped me dead in my tracks. I was a Labrador on a hunt, sniffing the air.

Denalyn was impressed. I don't typically notice new smells. The truth is, I don't notice anything. I have the observation skills of a mole. Denalyn can rearrange the furniture, and if she doesn't warn me, I'll plop down in the spot where there used to be a chair and end up on a coffee table. She's working on a book entitled *I Married a Caveman*. My brain has a weak detail-detection section. But that day it came to life.

"That fragrance is really nice," I told her.

The aroma wasn't the smell of food; she wasn't cooking. It wasn't perfume; she never wears it. It was, well, it was the fragrance of a forest on a cool fall morning. Then again, it made me think of a spice wagon at a market. Or was it the smell of the ocean? I couldn't isolate the source.

"Denalyn, did you buy some fresh flowers?"

She smiled. "No, I bought some oils."

Oils? I know oils. I'm the son of a mechanic. I've even been known to change the oil in our cars. "You bought some Valvoline?" That was the caveman speaking.

She produced a purse full of small bottles. Myrrh. Lavender. Cassia. Spikenard. Cinnamon. Sandalwood. You'd have thought she'd befriended a merchant in the back roads of Jerusalem. She had diffused them into our house. She had applied them to her skin. She had even put drops in her water.

"I've been putting some in yours as well." (The caveman hadn't noticed.)

Turns out she'd become quite the student of essential oils. They are considered the most ancient natural health product. For several thousand years people all over the world have been extracting these liquids from herbs, flowers, and fruits. Apparently they help us sleep, relax, digest, focus, and stay energized.

Do oils really help us? I'm no expert. But do oils help us understand the energizing power of the Holy Spirit? You bet your sweet cinnamon they do. Anointing with oil is often a symbol of the presence of God's Spirit.

Do you recall the story of David? "Samuel took the flask of olive oil he had brought and anointed David with the oil. And the Spirit of the LORD came powerfully upon David from that day on" (1 Sam. 16:13 NLT).

God gave this instruction to Elijah: "Anoint Elisha son of Shaphat from the town of Abel-meholah to replace you as my prophet" (1 Kings 19:16 NLT).

God instructed Moses, "Clothe your brother, Aaron, and his sons with these garments, and then anoint and ordain them. Consecrate them so they can serve as my priests. . . . Cleanse the altar by purifying it; make it holy by anointing it with oil" (Ex. 28:41; 29:36 NLT).

This worship stanza was offered to Jesus: "God . . . poured fragrant oil on your head, marking you out as king, far above your dear companions" (Heb. 1:9 THE MESSAGE).

Jesus began his ministry by announcing, "The Spirit of the Lord is upon me, because he has anointed me" (Luke 4:18).

Do you see the interplay between oil, anointing, and the Holy Spirit? Anointing oil is a metaphor for the Spirit of God. "Now it is God who makes both us and you stand firm in Christ. *He anointed us*, set his seal of ownership on us, and put his Spirit in our hearts as a deposit, guaranteeing what is to come" (2 Cor. 1:21–22 NIV, emphasis mine). God poured out upon you, not the oil my wife keeps in a drawer, but the power-providing, heart-healing oil of the Holy Spirit.

Your life has been consecrated, dedicated, and embrocated with the Spirit of God. Was this not God's promise?

> And in the last days it shall be, God declares,
> that I will pour out my Spirit on all flesh. (Acts 2:17)

The verb *pour* deserves to be highlighted. God does not distribute the Spirit with an eyedropper or a tablespoon. This is no suggestion of a dab, sprinkle, splash, or occasional drop. We are "saved . . . through the washing of . . . the Holy Spirit, whom he [God] *poured* out" (Titus 3:5–6 NIV, emphasis mine). He douses us with himself. He does to us what Moses was told to do with Aaron. "You shall take the anointing oil and pour it on his head and anoint him" (Ex. 29:7).

The era of this command was around 1300 BC. Two million Hebrews were finally free from Egyptian captivity. A civilization was being born. Through Moses, God instructed the Israelites on every detail of life, especially the details about the tabernacle, which foreshadowed the temple.

Aaron and his sons were selected to serve as priests. Their ordination could hardly have been more elaborate. Special headdresses, tunics, and clothing had been stitched together. And then, when everything was completed, God gave this instruction to Moses.

Take the finest spices: twelve pounds of liquid myrrh, half that amount (that is, six pounds) of sweet-smelling cinnamon, six pounds of sweet-smelling cane, and twelve pounds of cassia. Weigh all these by the Holy Place measure. Also take four quarts of olive oil, and mix all these things like a perfume to make a holy olive oil. This special oil must be put on people and things to make them ready for service to God. (Ex. 30:23–25 NCV)

I showed this passage to our resident oil expert. "Denalyn," I said, "let's replicate this concoction. Where can we buy twelve pounds of myrrh, six pounds of cinnamon, six pounds of cane, and twelve pounds of cassia?"

She gave me that I-married-a-caveman look and explained that the myrrh alone would cost $3,000.

Well, maybe we could at least calculate the amount used. We converted the Bible's measurements to liquid equivalents—gallons instead of pounds. Next we tallied the total amount of oil prescribed. It was roughly the equivalent of six gallons. I envisioned a five-gallon cooler that is emptied on the winning football coach. This was no small amount of oil.

Moses was told to pour it over the utensils of the tabernacle so they would be "soaked in holiness" (Ex. 30:29 THE MESSAGE).

Next came the anointing of Aaron and his sons. "The anointing oil . . . was poured over Aaron's head, . . . ran down his beard and onto the border of his robe" (Ps. 133:2 NLT). The man was marinated! Oil saturated his beard, seeped into the pores of his skin. It moistened his hair, rolled down the middle of his back, and dripped from the hem of his garment to the ground. His wife likely detected the fragrance from a block away. "We smelled you coming, Aaron."

The oil changed more than his scent; it demarcated his assignment. "Anoint Aaron and his sons and consecrate them so they may serve me as priests" (Ex. 30:30 NIV). They were consecrated for a purpose. They carried upon them God's special favor. They bore a unique authority. Can you imagine how they must have felt?

I so hope you can, because an even greater anointing has come upon you. Do you understand what happened on the day of your conversion? Yes, grace covered you. Yes, the tent of God's sovereignty was stretched over you. Yes, the pathway to heaven was laid out before you. And yes, yes, yes, you were anointed by the Holy Spirit. You have been consecrated for a holy work.

> But you have an anointing from the Holy One [you have been set apart, specially gifted and prepared by the Holy Spirit], and all of you know [the truth because He teaches us, illuminates our minds, and guards us from error]. (1 John 2:20 AMP)

From the perspective of heaven, the gift of the Spirit is the greatest gift imaginable. In a stunning statement Jesus told his followers that it was to their advantage for him to go away (John 16:7). His departure would trigger the arrival of the Spirit. I'm envisioning some furrowed brows on the faces of the disciples. What could be better than the presence of Jesus beside them? To be able to ask Jesus questions, to hear his teaching, to watch his actions. To have Jesus near you. Could anything be better?

Something could—the Spirit within you.

Jesus limited himself to a physical body. He could be in only one place at one time. The Holy Spirit, however, is unlimited. He can be everywhere all the time. Jesus was a regional force; the Spirit is a global force. There is no place that he is not!

> Where can I go from your Spirit?
>> Where can I flee from your presence?
> If I go up to the heavens, you are there;
>> if I make my bed in the depths, you are there. (Ps. 139:7–8 NIV)

God has so doused you with his Spirit that you will never be in a place where the Spirit is not. God has decreed you to be special to him. You are unique among people. You are part of his priesthood (1 Peter 2:5). He has soaked you with himself.

Bask in this blessing.

Don't grade yourself according to the inches of your waist, the square footage of your house, the color of your skin, the label on your clothing, the presence of awards, or the absence of pimples. You are above all that. You are not the sum total of your salary or your Instagram followers. Your value does not depend on the car you drive or the jewelry you wear. You've been anointed by the Holy Spirit. This anointing changes everything.

In the summer of 1871, two women of Dwight L. Moody's congregation felt an unusual burden to pray for him "that the Lord would give him the baptism of the Holy Ghost and of fire." Moody would see them praying in the front row of his church, and he was irritated. But soon he gave in, and in September he began to pray with them every Friday afternoon. He felt as though his ministry was becoming a sounding brass with little power. On November 24, 1871, Moody's church building was destroyed in the great Chicago fire. He went to New York to seek financial help. Day and night he would walk the streets, desperate for the touch of God's power in his life. Then suddenly . . .

one day, in the city of New York—oh, what a day!—I cannot describe it, I seldom refer to it; it is almost too sacred an experience to name. . . . I can only say that God revealed Himself to me, and I had such an experience of His love that I had to ask Him to stay His hand. I went to preaching again. The sermons were not different; I did not present any new truths, and yet hundreds were converted. I would not now be placed back where I was before that blessed experience if you should give me all the world—it would be as the small dust of the balance.[1]

God offers this anointing to all of us. When you pray, preach, prophesy, or live out your faith, you are empowered by the Holy Spirit's presence. Lean into him. You grow weary, but the Spirit never does. Your understanding is limited, but the Spirit has unsearchable wisdom. You cannot see the future, but the Spirit is as present in tomorrow as he is in today. You may be puzzled by circumstances, but the Spirit is never bewildered, befuddled, or confused. And because he is in you, you have power that you would never have had without him.

I leaned into this promise a couple of days ago. A dear friend spent an hour describing his frustration with his father. The two are in business together, and the father has made some questionable decisions. My friend was very aggravated. And I was confused. No money had been lost or opportunities squandered. Why was he so agitated?

I didn't know what to say, so as I listened, I prayed, *Lord, what is going on here? Why is my friend so bothered?*

A word came to my mind. *Grief. "That's it,"* I said to myself. And I told my friend, "You aren't angry at your dad. You are grieving his demise. The mantle is being transferred from his shoulders to yours. The truth is you are sad. You're going to miss him."

The words found their mark. My friend began to weep.

The Holy Spirit ministered through me. All I did was believe that the Spirit was present and trust that my anointing was sufficient for the task.

Do the same. The Spirit will give you whatever you need to do the holy work he has called you to do. Why was the ministry of Jesus so mighty? Because God gave him "the Spirit without measure" (John 3:34 NASB). Would God not do the same with us? He is no miser. He does not ration the Spirit in bits and pieces. He does not parcel himself upon us in increments. Scrooge? No. Generous? Yes.

Paul's prayer for the Ephesians is God's will for you: "I ask the

Father in his great glory to give you the power to *be strong inwardly through his Spirit*" (Eph. 3:16 NCV, emphasis mine).

Do not neglect your anointing. God set you apart for a special work. He poured his Spirit upon you! Receive him. Believe him. And leave oily footprints everywhere you go.

CHAPTER 10

The Coming Wave

The Spirit As a River of Living Water

I will pour out water for the thirsty land
and make streams flow on dry land.
I will pour out my Spirit into your children
and my blessing on your descendants.
Your children will grow like a tree in the grass,
like poplar trees growing beside streams of water.
—ISAIAH 44:3–4 NCV

A shadow has set upon American society. The Christian faith is in decline. Spiritual indifference is everywhere. Acquisition of property, increase of wealth, more possessions—this is what matters to people. They are obsessed with stuff and disinterested in God. Addiction is up. Church attendance is down. Even with the population booming as much as 300 percent in some areas over the last ten years, the largest religious denomination is reporting a decline in membership.

On the rare occasion that spirituality is discussed, the gospel is often under attack. The authority of the Bible is questioned. Universalism is suddenly in vogue. No one is a sinner. No one will be lost. Everyone will somehow be saved. There is no eternal punishment. The idea of judgment is archaic and barbaric.

This is not good news.

But this is not recent news. It sounds as though I'm describing the plight of modern-day America. Actually I'm portraying the spiritual landscape of eighteenth-century America.

Francis Asbury, a Methodist bishop, filed this gloomy report in 1794: "[In the American frontier] not one in a hundred came here to get religion, but rather to get plenty of good land." Andrew Fulton, a visiting Presbyterian missionary from Scotland, reported that in "all the newly formed towns in this western colony, there are few religious people."[1]

The nation was suffering from a spiritual drought. But then something wonderful happened. The rainfall of revival began to fall.

The first drops fell in Kentucky. The Cane Ridge Church met in an unassuming building on the side of a large hill. The pastor, a Presbyterian by the name of Barton W. Stone, was one of dozens of church leaders who had been praying for revival. They met regularly for prayer and called churches to gather for extended times of Communion.

One of these Eucharist events was held at Cane Ridge. The simple meetinghouse could accommodate some five hundred people. Anticipating a significant crowd, the leaders constructed a large tent. It quickly proved inadequate. People began arriving on August 6, 1801. It was estimated that between ten thousand and twenty-five thousand worshipers gathered over the next three days. They poured out of the hills. They arrived by wagon, on foot, on horseback. They listened to sermons, engaged in worship, received Communion, and experienced personal renewal. There was no shortage of weeping, groaning, and crying.

The Cane Ridge Communion, stated one historian, was "arguably . . . the most important religious gathering in all of American history."[2] "It ignited the explosion of evangelical religion, which soon reached into nearly every corner of American life. For decades the prayer of camp meetings and revivals across the land was 'Lord, make it like Cane Ridge.'"[3]

Spiritual revival broke out. During the first half of the nineteenth century, church attendance increased. Societal reforms began. The awakening contributed directly to the abolition of slavery and defense of women's rights.[4] The Second Great Awakening was born.

Do you ever aspire for such a move of God in our time? I do too. Christianity is on the decline in our country. The number of believers has dropped 12 percent in the last decade.[5] Our belief in God is down while our belief in ghosts is up.[6]

Thirty percent of millennials say they feel lonely. Of all the age groups surveyed, millennials feel most alone. Furthermore, 22 percent of millennials say they have zero friends.[7] The chapter of life that should be marked by possibilities and optimism is characterized by isolation.

Major depression is on the rise. The increase is found in all age groups but is rising fastest among teens and young adults.[8] Of all the statistics the increase in suicide is most alarming. According to federal data the US suicide rate is the highest it has been since World War II, up 33 percent since 1999.[9]

One friend told me that she has decided not to have children. She cannot bear the thought of the world her child would inherit. We understand her concern.

Yet we have this hope. Revival can come at any moment. At the right hour God will open the floodgate and release his Spirit like a flowing river into society. This was the promise of Jesus.

> On the last and most important day of the feast Jesus stood up and said in a loud voice, "Let anyone who is thirsty come to me and drink. If anyone believes in me, rivers of living water will flow out from that person's heart, as the Scripture says." Jesus was talking about the Holy Spirit. The Spirit had not yet been given, because Jesus had not yet been raised to glory. But later, those who believed in Jesus would receive the Spirit. (John 7:37–39 NCV)

Jesus spoke these words on an October day in a crowded Jerusalem. People had packed the streets for the Feast of Tabernacles, an annual reenactment of the rock-giving-water miracle of Moses. Each morning for seven days a priest filled a golden pitcher with water and carried it down a people-lined path to the temple. Announced by trumpets, the priest would, using a funnel, pour the water onto the base of the altar. Then on the last day, the great day, the priests gave the altar a Jericho loop—seven circles—dousing it with seven vessels of water.[10]

It may have been at this very moment that the rustic rabbi from the northlands commanded the people's attention. He stood up. Teachers typically sat down and spoke. Not this one. He had a major invitation to offer. He issued it with a "loud voice." "Drink me," he declared, "and living water will flow out of you!" And lest we miss the meaning of the moment, John (uncharacteristically) offered commentary on his own scripture. "Jesus was talking about the Holy Spirit."

Each word of his promise is precious! "If *anyone* is thirsty."[11] Skin color does not matter. Income level is of no importance. Background checks will not be made. There is only one qualification.

"If anyone is *thirsty*." Not "if anyone is worthy, qualified, trained, or mature." All that is needed is an admission of thirst. Who fails to meet this criterion? The teenager is thirsty for friends. The senior citizen is thirsty for hope. The heartbroken man is thirsty for a second chance. The shame-filled woman is thirsty for acceptance. We are thirsty—thirsty to be happy, thirsty to have meaning, thirsty for answers and strength. Thirsty.

"If anyone is thirsty," Jesus offers, "come to *me* and drink." Could his direction be clearer? Yet for all its clarity we succeed at muddling it. Jesus was speaking in the midst of an extremely religious moment. Even so he invited, "Come to *me*!" A person might attend a thousand religious events and not find refreshment for the soul. Spiritual thirst is quenched only by Christ himself.

The storytelling of C. S. Lewis is helpful here. In the Chronicles of Narnia series, a young girl named Jill enters a strange and wonderful country. After a time of wandering she looks for water. She is thirsty.

She finds a stream yet is hesitant to drink from the water because of the presence of a Lion. He asks if she is thirsty; she says that she is dying of thirst. "Then drink," the Lion offers. Yet she is afraid and asks if he would mind leaving while she drinks. She immediately realizes the presumption of her request.

She then asks the Lion to promise not to do anything to her if she draws near the stream. He explains that he makes no promises. Driven nearly frantic with thirst, she asks the Lion if he ever eats girls. He answers, "I have swallowed up girls and boys, women and men, kings and emperors, cities and realms."

She tells the Lion that she dares not come to the water and drink. He tells her that she will then die of thirst. She replies by saying that she will find another stream. He responds matter-of-factly, "There is no other stream."[12]

Christ is the only fount.

"Come to me and *drink*," he invites. Not sip. Not taste. Not sample. But gulp. Long, refreshing swallows of him. Consume Christ. To drink Jesus is to receive him into the driest parts of our lives. As we do, "rivers of living water will flow out."

As Jesus goes in, the Holy Spirit flows out. We become sources of living water to those around us.

I did not grow up on a ranch, but I was raised in the land of ranches. I learned that there are two ways to increase the value of ranchland: strike oil or discover water. If a ranch has a river or creek running through it or drillable water within it, it will be advertised as a ranch with "live water." It is blessed by a constant flow of H_2O. Livestock have water to drink. Farmers have water for irrigation. The presence of water changes dry ranchland into useful property.

The presence of Spirit-filled Christ followers does the same to society. We refresh. We soothe. We soften. The Holy Spirit flows out of us into the dry places of the world. This is how revival happens. We drink Christ and, consequently, leak life.

As Jesus goes in,
the Holy Spirit
flows out. We
become sources
of living water to
those around us.

This happened yesterday with my wife. While shopping for groceries, she noticed a mother being pushed in a wheelchair by her teenage children. The mother was frail and pale. An oxygen tube was wrapped beneath her nose.

Denalyn felt prompted to help her. But how? The answer came as Denalyn waited behind the mother in the checkout line. The Holy Spirit told Denalyn to pay for the woman's groceries. "Of course," Denalyn told me later. "I don't know why I didn't think of it sooner."

The shopper was surprised and grateful. Denalyn gave the payment, and the family said, "Thank you," and Denalyn was thrilled. She described the moment as the highlight of her day. (I thought waking up next to me would have been the highlight.) The act was unforced. It was genuine. It was not an obligation or a burden. You might say that it flowed out of her as water would flow out of a fountain.

Take that small event and multiply it by 2.3 billion, the number of Christians in the world.[13] Suppose each of us each day responded to the prompting of the Spirit to bless someone else. Acts of kindness. Words of encouragement. Might revival happen in our day?

This happened in 1801. What began in the Cane Ridge church spread across the frontier like a spring shower. Churches began to grow. Christians began to influence society.

Revivals cannot be forced, faked, or conjured up. Revival, as one man wrote, is a "strange and sovereign work of God in which He visits His own people, restoring, reanimating and releasing them into the fullness of His blessing."[14] By its power, writes another, "vast energies, hitherto slumbering, are awakened, and new forces—for long preparing under the surface—burst into being."[15]

Jonathan Edwards was a prime leader in the first Great Awakening in eighteenth-century America. He stated that initially a few sermons were preached, a few converts were made. "But then God in so remarkable a manner took the work into his own hands, and did as much in a day or two that, under normal circumstances took the entire Christian community, using every means at their disposal, with the blessing of God, more than a year to accomplish."[16]

That is called "rivers of living water."

Do we not long to see a mighty and mysterious work of God among his children?

Let's request one. Let's do so by imitating the prayer of the country preacher. He was so distraught by the conditions of the world that he went outside and drew a big circle in the dirt. He stood in the center of the circle and prayed, *Lord, bring revival and begin with everyone in this circle.*

Change begins when change begins with me.

Do we desire to see a new day? Then let's pray prayers like this one: *God, please release living water upon and through your children. Let us be sources of life and love everywhere we go. We want to be useful servants.*

One of the most famous revivals happened early in the twentieth century in Wales. One hundred thousand people came to Christ in less than a year.[17]

Almost empty bars were closed for lack of business. Magistrates saw their courts emptied of criminals. Miners even had to retrain the mules that worked in the coal mines. Many of the animals had been trained to respond to vulgar commands. But when the men got cleaned up, their language did as well, and the mules had to learn a new vocabulary.[18]

May the need arise to retrain some mules today.

Let the thirsty souls come. Let them come to Christ. And let the rivers of living water flow again.

CHAPTER 11

Speak Up

The Spirit As Tongues of Fire

But how shall they ask him to save them unless they believe in him?
And how can they believe in him if they have never heard about
him? And how can they hear about him unless someone tells them?
—Romans 10:14 TLB

Then Peter stood up with the Eleven, raised his voice and
addressed the crowd: "Fellow Jews and all of you who live
in Jerusalem, let me explain this to you; listen carefully
to what I say. . . . Repent and be baptized, every one of
you, in the name of Jesus Christ for the forgiveness of
your sins. And you will receive the gift of the Holy Spirit.
The promise is for you and your children and for all who
are far off—for all whom the Lord our God will call.
—Acts 2:14, 38–39 NIV

What's gotten into Peter?

Seven weeks ago he was hiding because of Jesus; today he is proclaiming salvation through Jesus. In the hours before the cross, he denied Christ. Now he is announcing Christ. On the eve of Good Friday, you couldn't get him to speak up. Today you can't get him to shut up!

What's gotten into Peter?

He was a coward at the crucifixion. A question from a servant girl undid him. He wasn't bludgeoned by a soldier or intimidated by the Sanhedrin. Rome didn't threaten to extradite him. No, a waitress from the downtown diner heard his accent and asked if he knew Jesus. Peter panicked. Meltdown. He not only denied his Lord; he bleeped the very idea. "Then Peter began to place a curse on himself and swear, 'I don't know the man'" (Matt. 26:74 NCV).

But look at him on the Day of Pentecost, declaring to a throng of thousands, "God has made Jesus—the man you nailed to the cross—both Lord and Christ" (Acts 2:36 NCV). Gutsy language. Lynch mobs feed on such accusations. The same crowd that shouted, "Crucify him!" could crucify him.

From wimp to warrior in fifty days. What happened?

Oh, how we need to know. We admire the Pentecost Peter yet identify with the Passover one. Our convictions wrinkle and resolve melts. We determine to do better but struggle. We make promises and fail to keep them.

We look at other believers and ask, Why is her life so fruitful and mine so fruitless? Why is his life so powerful and mine so weak? Aren't we saved by the same Christ? Don't we read the same Scripture and rally around the same cross? Why do some look like the early Peter and others the later? Or, more to the point, Why do I vacillate between the two in any given week?

Jesus embedded an answer in his final earthly message. He told Peter and the other followers, "Wait here to receive the promise from the Father which I told you about. John baptized people with water, but in a few days you will be baptized with the Holy Spirit" (Acts 1:4–5 NCV).

One hundred and twenty of them gathered. The apostles, minus Judas, plus Matthias, his replacement; Mary, the mother of Jesus; the brothers of Jesus: James, Joseph, Simon, and Judas.[1] Mary Magdalene perhaps? Joanna the wife of Chuza and Susanna, no doubt. They followed Jesus. Certainly they were charter members of his church.

Jesus sent them to Jerusalem to wait, and they went and waited.

They did not know for how long. A day? A decade? Nor did they know exactly for what they were waiting. For the power of the Holy Spirit, sure . . . but in what form, in what way? Could they have imagined what would happen?

"When the day of Pentecost came, they were all together in one place" (Acts 2:1 NIV). Pentecost was one of the three feast days on which all the Jewish men were required to appear in Jerusalem at least once in their lifetime. Many had arrived more than fifty days earlier and participated in the Passover celebration. They came from all over the then-known world. Jews from Persia. Medes with long, curled beards and thick, plaited black hair. Poor Jews from Arabia in simple robes. Proud Jews from Rome in their togas. Jerusalem's population may have swelled from a hundred thousand to a million.[2] A dozen dialects echoed in the markets. Coins from every currency jingled in the purses of the merchants.

The city of David hummed with activity.

The divine timing was precise. Now, with the sacrifice of Christ accomplished. Now, with the tomb of Christ vacated. Now, with the person of Christ ascended to heaven's throne. Now, with the apostles gathered in one place, in prayer, awaiting the power of the Spirit. Now, with representatives of at least fifteen nations gathered in one city . . . It was time.

> Suddenly a sound like the blowing of a violent wind came from heaven and filled the whole house where they were sitting. They saw what seemed to be tongues of fire that separated and came to rest on each of them. All of them were filled with the Holy Spirit and began to speak in other tongues as the Spirit enabled them.
>
> Now there were staying in Jerusalem God-fearing Jews from every nation under heaven. When they heard this sound, a crowd came together in bewilderment, because each one heard their own language being spoken. (Acts 2:2–6 NIV)

The Spirit came "suddenly" and "from heaven" (v. 2). There is no question as to the source and surprise of the Spirit. The gift came "where they were sitting" (v. 2). A subtle reminder of the Spirit as a gift, perhaps? Luke could have said "where they were praying," "worshiping," or "calling out to God." But the emphasis is on the sovereign Spirit, not on the activity of the followers.

"What seemed to be tongues of fire" descended and "came to rest on each of them" (v. 3). "All of them were filled" (v. 4). Because of the Holy Spirit, each one could speak with such power that people from all over the world heard the story of Jesus in "their own language" (v. 6).

What a moment that must have been! Andrew declaring the goodness of God in the tongue of the Egyptians. Thomas recounting the miracles of Jesus in the dialect of Cappadocia. Mary the Mother of Jesus describing the birth of Jesus to a group from Crete in the language of their land.

Babel was, for a moment, reversed.

Some bystanders were cynical, accusing the disciples of early morning inebriation in need of Breathalyzing. But others were amazed and asked, "Whatever could this mean?" (v. 12 NKJV).

Good question. Crowded city. Prayerful followers. Rushing wind and falling fire. Fifteen nations represented in one assembly. Disciples speaking like trained translators of the United Nations. Whatever could this mean?

At least this: compelling communication was the first fruit of the Holy Spirit. He empowered and empowers Christ followers to declare the wonders of God in the heart languages of the world.

In time the Spirit would empower the first followers to heal the sick. In time he would direct them to lead the church. In time they would even raise the dead and pray open prison doors. But before all those mighty acts of power, there were mighty words of proclamation. "Unschooled, ordinary" (Acts 4:13 NIV) men and women were able to speak in languages they had never studied and impact nations they had never visited. Fire fell from heaven and melted the ice in about three thousand hearts (Acts 2:41).

God's will for his church has not changed.

Jesus told his followers, "Do not be anxious how you are to speak or what you are to say, for what you are to say will be given to you in that hour. For it is not you who speak, but the Spirit of your Father speaking through you" (Matt. 10:19–20).

Best I can tell, this promise has not been rescinded.

Nor has this one: "But when the Holy Spirit has come upon you, you will receive power to testify about me with great effect" (Acts 1:8 TLB).

I could use the life of Billy Graham as an example. He was the son of a North Carolina dairy farmer who in his lifetime told more than a billion people about Christ.

I could use Charles Spurgeon as an example. This nineteenth-century preacher from London declared God's Word in such a manner that people still study his sermons a century and a half later.

I could use Mother Teresa as an example. Scarcely five feet tall, she stood as a giant among orators of the faith.

I could tell you stories about legends like Graham, Spurgeon, and Mother Teresa, but I'd rather tell you about Brenda Jones.

On the day she went to see the plastic surgeon, she was in a battle with breast cancer. The purpose of the consultation was to discuss breast reconstruction. Yet she did what she often did. She changed the topic. She wanted to tell her doctor what Jesus had done for her.

Brenda asked if she could share a story. Dr. Pete politely said yes. She proceeded to tell him about her hope for heaven. She didn't want to die, she explained, but death to her was a necessary step from this life to the next.

Pete was intrigued. He was at the top of his professional ladder, but it was leaning against the wrong building. He crossed his arms and listened. He listened to the story about the God who became a baby, then a man, and then a sacrifice for humanity. "He died for you, Doctor," she told him.

Here was a frail, diseased woman talking to a highly educated, nationally recognized surgeon, telling him about his sin and need for a Savior. The fifteen-minute conversation changed him forever. I baptized Pete soon thereafter on a cold January day in an outdoor swimming pool. (I dedicated this book to Pete—Dr. Pete Ledoux.)

Then there is the story of Brazilian pastor Antenor Goncalves. He has served a congregation in Itu, Brazil, for more than two decades. I've heard him teach, both in English and in Portuguese. I could listen to him preach for hours. But he would have no story to tell were it not for a blackboard on a porch.

His father saw it every day on the way to work. Antenor's dad took a train into the city, disembarked, and walked a couple of miles to his office in São Paulo. His commute took him through a modest neighborhood. A certain homeowner had turned his small porch into a billboard of sorts by placing a blackboard on it. Each morning he wrote a different scripture on the board. Each morning Mr. Goncalves paused to read the scripture of the day. Little by little the unspoken words touched his heart.

Words like these: *"Porque Deus amou o mundo de tal maneira que deu o seu Filho unigênito, para que todo aquele que nele crê não pereça, mas tenha a vida eterna"* (João 3:16).[3]

The words intrigued Mr. Goncalves. One day his curiosity got the better of him, or rather the Spirit took hold of him, and he knocked on the door of the house of the man with the blackboard. A conversation ensued and then an invitation to church and a Bible study. Soon Mr. Goncalves became a Christian.

Antenor was only two years old at the time. God used a blackboard to deliver a message that changed the course of his young life.

And he used a second-string quarterback to touch mine. Mike and I played on the same high school football team. More specifically we sat on the same bench. Neither of us was good enough to make the starting lineup. I was the backup center. Mike was the backup quarterback. We did what backups do. We stood on the sidelines.

And we did what teenage boys tend to do. In our case what we did was the opposite of what Christian boys tend to do.

Mike had an excuse. He wasn't a Christian. I was. But I wasn't living like one.

But then something happened. Mike met Pam. Pam knew Christ. Mike fell in love with Pam. Mike fell in love with Christ. And Mike began to change.

He treated people differently. He was at peace. There was a happy soberness about him. I noticed. At first I chalked up the change to romance. But even when Mike and Pam broke up a time or two, Mike's heart never changed.

Mike said few words to me about Jesus. Then again, he spoke to me each and every day. His respect for his teachers. His kindness toward others. He was a walking sermon. A few years later, five years to be exact, the example of Mike emboldened me to make a similar change in my life.

How do we explain the impact of these people? A spoken word to a doctor. A scribbled scripture on a blackboard. The contagious example of a friend. Advanced techniques of persuasion? Hardly. There is only one explanation.

The promise of Pentecost. The Spirit turns common folk into uncommon forces.

As Jesus explained, "[The Holy Spirit] will convict the world of sin" and "guide you into all truth" (John 16:8, 13 NKJV). The Holy Spirit takes our tongues of flesh and renders them tongues of fire. The Holy Spirit makes communication his priority. He is mentioned fifty-seven times in the book of Acts. Of those occasions he speaks through someone to someone else thirty-six times![4]

Might the Spirit do the same with us?

With you?

> The Spirit turns common folk into uncommon forces.

There is something unique about your story. No one else has your experience. No one else in all the history of the world has walked the path you have journeyed. Would you be willing to share it?

Here is an idea. Become well versed in your Ebenezer.

No, I'm not talking about a Charles Dickens character named Scrooge. I'm referring to your scrapbook of "only God" moments. Those precious events in your life that only God could have orchestrated.

The word *Ebenezer* appears in the context of the Hebrew people in the early days of their existence as a nation. God blessed them with deliverance from Egypt, a new identity, and a covenant. They saw plagues on enemies, holy fire in the sky, manna on their plates, and sandals that never wore out. Yet let one problem surface, and they wanted to scurry back to Egypt. They once melted down some earrings, made a cow, and began to pray to it.

Really?

How quickly they forgot.

Over the years, however, they developed ways to remember. One of the ways was called the Ebenezer stone, or "stone of help." After a particularly resounding victory in battle as well as a spiritual renewal, they set up a stone to symbolize God's faithfulness (1 Sam. 7:12). The Ebenezer stone was a tangible reminder of what God had done for them. The Israelites would show the stone to their neighbors and to their children as a way to recount God's faithfulness.

What are your Ebenezer moments?

Not everyone can evangelize like Billy Graham, write like Charles Spurgeon, or care for the poor like Mother Teresa. But don't you think we each can talk about our "only God" moments?

There was an occasion when Jesus healed a deranged man. The fellow had made his home in a cemetery and cut himself with rocks. When Jesus delivered him from the affliction, the man wanted to go with Jesus. Christ, however, gave this instruction: "Go home to your friends, and tell them what great things the Lord has done for you, and how He has had compassion on you" (Mark 5:19 NKJV).

In other words speak up. Show someone your Ebenezer stone.

God's plan is reduced

to one strategy:

ordinary folks telling

the extraordinary

story of Jesus with the

extraordinary power

of the Holy Spirit.

Do you feel ill-equipped to do so? That's okay. You have God's Spirit to help you. God's plan is reduced to one strategy: ordinary folks telling the extraordinary story of Jesus with the extraordinary power of the Holy Spirit.

People like Samuel Justin, an unassuming preacher in India. In a season of great persecution and rising fear, the police came to his house. They demanded that he answer their questions. At one point one of the officers took out a notebook and mentioned many of the things that were happening.

The official then asked the question, "Now by what authority are you doing these things?" In this potentially fearful moment God had given an opening. Samuel fetched his Bible and read this passage to the policeman: "Then Jesus came to them and said, 'All authority in heaven and on earth has been given to me.'" The officer solemnly took notes about this Jesus and his authority.

Samuel continued to read: "Therefore go and make disciples of all nations, baptizing them in the name of the Father and of the Son and of the Holy Spirit." The officer continued to record the words in his investigation notebook: "And teaching them to obey everything I have commanded you. And surely I am with you always, to the very end of the age."[5]

The officer said he would take this report to his supervisors and share by whose authority Samuel did his work. From that point on the police officers did not bother the church and even provided some protection for them in the work of spreading the good news.[6]

Always remember by whose authority you do this work, my friend. Pray with confidence. Preach in power. Counsel as one who knows the counsel of heaven and the Counselor, the Holy Spirit.

CHAPTER 12

You Unleashed

The Spirit As the Gift Giver

When he went up to the heights, he led a parade
of captives, and he gave gifts to people.
—Ephesians 4:8 NCV

In August 2005 the entire nation watched in shock as Hurricane Katrina devastated the city of New Orleans, Louisiana. Who would have thought we would ever hear these words on a news report? "Today about 20,000 refugees were moved from the Superdome in New Orleans to the Astrodome in Houston."

Entire neighborhoods were left sitting beneath twenty feet of water. Citizens hacked their way onto roofs in hopes of being rescued via helicopters. Residents sought refuge in nearby cities. New Orleans came to San Antonio in the form of 12,500 evacuees.

It just so happened that a good friend of mine was placed in charge of our local refugee center. A large downtown warehouse became a triage site. As I toured the center with Robert, I was struck by one fact: every volunteer had an assignment.

Some people distributed blankets. Others handed out sandwiches. A covey of medical professionals examined people with health concerns. Counselors and pastors counseled the suddenly displaced. My friend handed me a folding chair and pointed to a long line of forlorn victims. "Make yourself useful," he said. "Go pray and listen."

I did.

The image of that warehouse came to mind as I was reviewing one of the most inspiring, convicting, and controversial of the Holy Spirit metaphors: the gift giver. It seems to me that the entire world is in a state of trauma.

People do not know why they were born or where they are destined to go. This is the age of much know-how and very little know-why. The invisible enemy of sin and secularism has left us dazed and bewildered. In the midst of the wreckage sits God's intended rescue center, the church. We provide a haven for hurting people, a safe place to come in out of the storm. We each have responsibilities, and when we work together, the displaced find a place. And, behind it all, overseeing the operation is the Holy Spirit.

And he does this through the distribution of spiritual gifts. "Now to each one the manifestation of the Spirit is given for the common good. . . . All [spiritual gifts] are the work of one and the same Spirit, and he distributes them to each one, just as he determines" (1 Cor. 12:7, 11 NIV).

The Holy Spirit is the ultimate gift giver. He garnishes his children with supernatural abilities that glorify God, bless the needy, and edify the church. Would it not be a tragedy of the highest order to miss out on your unique-to-you assignment? That was the opinion of Paul, the apostle.

> Now concerning spiritual gifts, brethren, I do not want you to be ignorant: . . . There are diversities of gifts, but the same Spirit. There are differences of ministries, but the same Lord. And there are diversities of activities, but it is the same God who works all in all. But the manifestation of the Spirit is given to each one for the profit of all." (1 Cor. 12:1, 4–7 NKJV)

The Holy Spirit is the
ultimate gift giver. He
garnishes his children
with supernatural
abilities that glorify
God, bless the needy,
and edify the church.

Christ gives gifts to his church. The Spirit is his authorized distributor. While the gifts are diverse, their goal is singular: the common good of the community. The Corinthians had forgotten this. Spiritual gifts were dividing the church. Some people were showing off. Others were jealous. Everyone was confused. So Paul tried to clear things up by describing some possible gifts.

> For to one is given the word of wisdom through the Spirit, to another the word of knowledge through the same Spirit, to another faith by the same Spirit, to another gifts of healings by the same Spirit, to another the working of miracles, to another prophecy, to another discerning of spirits, to another different kinds of tongues, to another the interpretation of tongues. But one and the same Spirit works all these things, distributing to each one individually as He wills. (1 Cor. 12:8–11 NKJV)

Keep a few things in mind as you review this scripture.

NO GIFT LIST IS COMPLETE. The New Testament has at least five: 1 Corinthians 12:8–10; 1 Corinthians 12:28–30; Romans 12:6–8; Ephesians 4:11–12; 1 Peter 4:10–11. It was not the intent of the apostle, in any of the epistles, to create an exhaustive list. This is proved by the fact that no two lists are identical. They are suggestive of the type of work the Holy Spirit does.

NOT ALL GIFTS ARE GIVEN AT THE MOMENT OF CONVERSION. If a person received all their gifts upon conversion, there would be no call to "eagerly desire gifts of the Spirit" (1 Cor. 14:1 NIV). Part of the excitement of living in step with the Spirit is to expect further equipping.

SPIRITUAL GIFTS ARE EXACTLY THAT, GIFTS. When the apostle Paul used the phrase "gifts of the Spirit," he nearly always used the Greek term *charisma* or *charismata*. A "charisma" is a gift in the purest sense of the word. You receive it, but you don't deserve it, and you certainly do not earn it. It is purely by the grace of God that the Spirit gives supernatural empowerments to believers.

SPIRITUAL GIFTS ARE NOT AN INDEX OF SPIRITUAL MATURITY. The Corinthian church had all the gifts (1 Cor. 1:4–8) but were lacking in Christian character. They clustered around personalities (1:10–17; 3:1–23), tolerated immorality (5:1–13), litigated against each other (6:1–11), abused the Lord's Supper (11:17–34), and used worship for self-promotion (12–14). The presence of gifts requires the maturity to use them wisely.

NATURAL TALENTS AND SPIRITUAL GIFTS ARE NOT ALWAYS IDENTICAL. Natural gifts advance personal causes; spiritual gifts advance God's cause. Your spiritual gift is often a divine application of your natural strength. Paul, for example, taught powerfully before his conversion. On the Damascus road Christ requisitioned the teaching strength for his purpose. If you managed people before following Christ, you will likely manage people after following Christ. Then again, the Holy Spirit might grant you a new gift altogether. What matters is this:

SPIRITUAL GIFTS EXIST TO EXALT CHRIST, EDIFY THE CHURCH, AND BLESS THE NEEDY. Gifts are not for personal and individual aggrandizement. They are to be used to build up the church.

My four-year-old granddaughter, Rosie, had an announcement for me the other day. "Papa Max, I know how to sing harmony."

"Wonderful," I replied, "let's sing together."

"Oh, no," she refused. "I like to sing harmony all by myself."

Someday she will learn that harmony requires the blending of multiple voices. Churches must learn the same. The Holy Spirit has given each of us a part in the wondrous song of grace. But we were not made to sing alone. Only when we blend our gifts can we expect a beautiful sound. Toward that end Paul went into detail about the types of gifts and the right way to use them.

They can be clustered this way:[1]

THE DISCERNING GIFTS. "To one is given the word of wisdom through

The Holy Spirit has
given each of us a part
in the wondrous song
of grace. But we were
not made to sing alone.
Only when we blend
our gifts can we expect
a beautiful sound.

the Spirit, to another the word of knowledge . . . to another discerning of spirits" (1 Cor. 12:8, 10 NKJV).

A *word of wisdom* is a message of appropriate counsel rightly suited for the occasion. Many years ago I had the opportunity to attend a pastors' conference. One of the teachers was a seasoned professor. I was sharing a dinner table with him one evening when he, somewhat abruptly, asked for the attention of the young ministers. "I have this word for you. Never sacrifice your family on the altar of Christian ministry." Having said it, he returned his attention to his meal. He made no further comment. Yet I never forgot the admonition. The Holy Spirit gave him a word of wisdom, and he, in turn, blessed us.

He may use you to do the same. When you sense the Spirit has an important message for you to share, share it! Don't assume that people already know what you know. God might very well be using you to convey an important truth in the triage system of the church.

A *word of knowledge* is a gift of information that a person has no way of knowing apart from the Holy Spirit. When Jesus told the Samaritan woman that she was living with a man who was not her husband and had been married to five other men before him, this was a word of knowledge (John 4:17–18).

Included in this grouping would be *the discerning of spirits* (1 Cor. 12:10 NKJV). The apostle Paul demonstrated this gift in a city called Philippi. The owners of a certain slave girl were making money from her fortune-telling. "Paul, greatly annoyed, turned and said to the spirit, 'I command you in the name of Jesus Christ to come out of her.' And he came out that very hour" (Acts 16:18 NKJV).

My wife has this gift. We were walking through a downtown area the other day when she saw a sign inviting people to walk in for a palm reading. She stopped, stared at the door, and declared, "Lord Jesus, shut that business down!" I haven't gone back to check on the status of the store, but I would advise against any financial investment in it.

In addition to the discerning gifts, Paul mentions:

THE DYNAMIC GIFTS. "To another faith by the same Spirit, to another gifts of healing by the same Spirit, to another the working of miracles" (1 Cor. 12:9–10 NKJV).

To have the *gift of faith* is to enjoy a sense of supernatural, contagious confidence. The Spirit uses this person to comfort the afflicted and bless the fearful.

Gifts of healing include the choice of the Spirit to render restoration through the prayers of a saint. This healing might be physical, emotional, or relational, but it is supernatural.

And then there is the *working of miracles*. God alters circumstances. He can reverse a financial downfall. He can soften the hard heart of a spouse. He can gain entryway into a closed nation. He is a miracle-working God, and he uses his servants to accomplish his will.

A third type of gifts are these:

THE DECLARATIVE GIFTS. "To another prophecy, . . . to another speaking in different kinds of tongues, and to still another the interpretation of tongues" (1 Cor. 12:10 NIV).

Paul explains the meaning of prophesy two chapters later. "He who prophesies speaks edification and exhortation and comfort" (1 Cor. 14:3 NKJV). To *prophesy* is to build up and encourage. A prophet may foretell the future but certainly foretells good news. Paul saw this as the most important gift. Not because the prophet is more important but because the task is so essential (1 Cor. 14:1).

Speaking in tongues and *interpretation of tongues* are magnificent, yet often controversial, gifts. There are two types of tongues described in the New Testament.

The first type was on display on the day the church was born. On that day people from at least fifteen nations heard the apostles speak in their own native languages. "And how is it that we hear, each of us in his own native language?" (Acts 2:8). God has a white-hot passion to see the gospel preached in every language and goes to supernatural lengths to see it done.

Paul was referring to a different expression of tongues when he wrote to the Corinthians. He said, "One who speaks in a tongue speaks not to men but to God; for no one understands him, but he utters mysteries in the Spirit" (1 Cor. 14:2). This language is understood by God, not by people (vv. 2, 28). Indeed, understanding it would require a person with the spiritual gift of interpretation.

The apostle Paul enjoyed this gift. He gave us a peek into his prayer life when he wrote:

So, when you pray in your private prayer language, don't hoard the experience for yourself. Pray for the insight and ability to bring others into that intimacy. If I pray in tongues, my spirit prays but my mind lies fallow, and all that intelligence is wasted. So what's the solution? The answer is simple enough. Do both. I should be spiritually free and expressive as I pray, but I should also be thoughtful and mindful as I pray. (1 Cor. 14:13–15 THE MESSAGE)

Paul enjoyed two types of prayer: praying with the spirit and praying with the mind (v. 15). Both were valuable. He prayed in tongues so frequently that he could say to a church who treasured this gift that he did so more than any of them (v. 18). Yet in public worship he "would rather speak five words with . . . understanding . . . than ten thousand words in a tongue" (v. 19 NKJV). What he did not do was engage, or instruct the church to engage, in only one form of prayer. The apostle sought to regulate, rather than denigrate, the practice of a heavenly language.

Let me pause and ask a question. How does this discussion of gifts strike you? Does it seem a bit, hmmm, what is the word, *supernatural*? It should. It is! The church is the supernatural expression of

God on the planet. He operates in ways beyond ours. Let's welcome this mysterious work of heaven in the church.

Forty years of ministry has left me convinced: we do not have what it takes to heal this hurting world. We might create programs, train staff, and build wonderful sanctuaries. But I'd gladly exchange them all for one raindrop from the Spirit of heaven.

We need his help.

One of the great tragedies of the last century has been the division of the church over the existence of spiritual gifts such as tongues and miracles. Many God-fearing Christians are convinced that these powerful gifts were discontinued when the apostles died. I know this line of reasoning well. I was among its adherents.

For the first ten years of my ministry, I taught that these more demonstrative gifts served only to launch the church. They were distributed by the apostles and then discontinued when the church was established, the Scriptures were written, and the apostles had passed into heaven.

My mind began to change in my midthirties. I wondered, *Where does a New Testament author ever say that certain gifts will cease upon completion of Scripture?* I found none. Indeed, Scripture urges us to earnestly desire spiritual gifts and not forbid speaking in tongues (1 Cor. 14:1, 39).

What about the belief that only the apostles could distribute the gifts, and with their deaths the miracles were discontinued? There is no direct statement to this effect. We see nonapostles like Ananias (Acts 9) blessing Saul with the Spirit. Besides, if only the apostles could give such gifts, why do we not see in the book of Acts a record of apostles traveling from church to church, laying hands on as many people as possible?

What's more, we don't assume that the more "mundane" gifts, like administration and service, were discontinued with the passing of the apostles. Isn't it arbitrary to suppose that the gift of hospitality is still valid, but the gift of tongues is not? Paul made it clear that he expected the gifts to remain in use until the return of Jesus: "You [Corinthians] are not lacking in any gift, as you wait for the revealing of our Lord Jesus Christ" (1 Cor. 1:7).

Most convincing of all (at least to me) is the fact the Holy Spirit chose to grace me with some of the very gifts I once discounted. He has healed people through my prayers. I've lost count of the number of parents whose infertility was reversed after I prayed for them. Apparently I have a pregnancy ministry.

I have spoken words of wisdom. Midway into a sermon I will often sense an impression to add or emphasize a point. I've come to expect that someone will repeat the impromptu remark and say, "That really touched me."

One of the most surprising gifts came to me at the age of sixty-four. Over a period of several months, I asked Jesus for a greater filling of his Spirit. I requested that he not hold back, that he pour out on me all the gifts he ever ordained me to have. In the predawn hours of a summer morning as I sat on our veranda and prayed, I began to experience a heavenly prayer language. From deep within me there welled a flow of utterances, staccato-like syllables. The feeling was one of delight and worship. This intimacy has continued each morning, indeed several times each day. I can always start it. I can always stop it. But I never want to.

This gift does not make me more important or special. I do not glow in the dark or levitate above trees. In fact, I've chuckled at the possibility that the Spirit helps me pray because my prayers are so scattered. I welcome his assistance.

I also welcome the regular reminder. Our God dwells in a supernatural realm. The unseen and miraculous are his stock-in-trade.

Donald Barnhouse, a well-respected pastor and scholar, studied at Princeton Theological Seminary. Twelve years after his graduation the school invited him to speak in their chapel service. Addressing one's

> Our God dwells in a supernatural realm. The unseen and miraculous are his stock-in-trade.

alma mater is difficult enough, but his Hebrew professor added to the fright by sitting near the front. After hearing the message the professor congratulated Barnhouse on a job well done and left him with these interesting words:

"I am glad that you are a big-godder. When my boys come back, I come to see if they are big-godders or little-godders, and then I know what their ministry will be." Barnhouse asked him to explain.

"Well, some men have a little God and they are always in trouble with Him. He can't do any miracles. He can't take care of the inspiration and transmission of the Scripture to us. He doesn't intervene on behalf of His people. They have a little God and I call them little-godders. Then there are those who have a great God. He speaks and it is done. He commands and it stands fast. He knows how to show Himself strong on behalf of them that fear Him. You, Donald, have a great God; and he will bless your ministry." He paused a moment, smiled, said, "God bless you," and walked out.[2]

We have a big God. The Holy Spirit is directing the church in extraordinary ways. What would happen if each believer identified and employed his or her Spirit-given gift? What if we, each one of us, operated according to the prompting and provision of the Spirit?

Receive Paul's admonition: "Do not be ignorant about spiritual gifts."

What has the Spirit gifted you to do? God did not place you on this earth to waste away your life in labor that does not employ your strengths. "Make a careful exploration of who you are and the work you have been given, and then sink yourself into that" (Gal. 6:4 THE MESSAGE).

Years ago I heard a fable about a dying father and his three sons. Having given his life to building a company, it was time to turn it over to one of them. But which one? The father had a plan. He called them to his bedside and handed a dollar bill to each young man and gave this assignment: "Buy something that fills the room. The one who takes up the most space will be entrusted with the company."

Each of the boys obeyed the instructions. The first returned with two bales of hay that he purchased for fifty cents apiece. They covered the floor of the room. The second produced two feather pillows, cut them open, and let the feathers fill the air. The father was pleased but not satisfied. He turned to the third son and asked, "What did you do with your dollar?"

The boy had nothing in his hands, so he explained: "I gave fifty cents to an orphanage, twenty cents to a church, and twenty cents to a soup kitchen."

One of his siblings objected. "But he did nothing to fill up the room."

"Yes, I did," the boy explained. "I spent the last dime on two items." He reached into his pocket and took out a little matchbook and candle. He lit the candle and turned off the light switch. From corner to corner the candle filled the room, not with hay or feathers, but with light.

With what are you filling your world?

CHAPTER 13

Breath on Bones

The Spirit As Breath

The Spirit gives life.
—2 Corinthians 3:6 ncv

We weren't yet teenagers. Close, but not quite. Barely in middle school. Unwhiskered. Pimpled. A bit awkward and probably in need of some discipline. Three of us boys comprised the entirety of a Bible class at church. Our teacher devised a plan that, I suppose, was intended to develop our leadership skills.

We paid Sunday evening visits to elderly folks who were unable to attend morning church services. Shut-ins, we called them. Health issues and aging bodies had left these people shut in and unable to get out.

Most of our visits took place in a small and rather unfavorably fragrant convalescent home on the outskirts of our small town. The patients seemed happy to see the church deacon and his young disciples. Our liturgy was a simple one. We stood in a horseshoe around the foot of each bed. The teacher would share a brief lesson. One of us would read a scripture. Another would say a prayer. If requested, we sang a hymn. And we would serve Communion. We traveled with a small box of wafers, grape juice, and cups.

A good way for young men to spend a Sunday evening. Right?

But then came the case of the sleeping grandpa. I do not recall why the teacher wasn't with us. I do recall that we were flying solo. Someone deposited us at the front door of the convalescent home. We divided up the responsibilities. One to say the prayer. One to read a scripture, and yours truly was left with the Communion kit.

We were the Protestant version of altar boys.

All went well until we encountered the slumbering man. He was in his bed, flat on his back with mouth open. The TV volume was loud, but his snoring was louder. "Sir," we said. No response. One of us touched his shoulder. Another gave him a shake. He just snorted.

We didn't think to ask a nurse for help. Turning and leaving was unacceptable. How dare we shirk our task?

So as the television roared and the old man snored, we did our duty. Prayer. Scripture, and, well, it was my turn. My friends looked at me. I looked at the man. His face was drawn, hair was gray, and mouth still wide open.

I did the only thing I knew to do. I placed a wafer on his tongue and washed it down with a cup of grape juice. We turned and scurried out of the room. He slept through the whole thing.

We've been known to do the same. We grow drowsy in our spirituality. Vibrancy is replaced by lethargy. Enthusiasm fades, and, well, we doze off. I'm not talking about hard-hearted rebels or cynics who reject God. I'm talking about the good-hearted saints who experience a dry heart, a waning love—who feel a disconnect in their relationship with God.

I may be talking about you.

If so, can I tell you some good news?

The mightiest force on the planet is here to help you. "The Spirit gives life" (John 6:63 NIV). Could Jesus have stated the mission of the Spirit more clearly? When the Godhead divvied up the assignments for humanity, the Father chose protection and provision, the Son took salvation—and the Spirit? He chose life distribution.

Life! Robust. Resilient. Happy hearted and hope filled. Isn't that what we need?

The Spirit gives it.

Need proof? Meet Ezekiel.

He was a radical, wide-eyed prophet who served as a thorn in the collective side of Israel during the sixth century BC. He was ever on the Hebrews' case, urging them to turn away from foreign idols and toward their living God (Ezek. 14:6). They did not listen. Consequently the nation experienced utter annihilation at the hands of the Babylonians in 587 BC. The city of Jerusalem was ransacked, and the magnificent temple was destroyed. Envision Washington, DC, lying in smoke and embers, the capitol building demolished and the White House burned down. The once-proud Hebrews were marched out of their homeland. From their exile in Babylonia the Jews declared, "Our bones are dried up, and our hope has gone. We are destroyed" (Ezek. 37:11 NCV).

The psalmist could only lament, "By the waters of Babylon, there we sat down and wept, when we remembered Zion" (Ps. 137:1). And again, "How shall we sing the LORD's song in a foreign land?" (v. 4).

The exile was a catastrophe.

But God had other plans. The people may have abandoned God, but God never abandoned them. He made the Hebrews a promise.

For here's what I'm going to do: I'm going to take you out of these countries, gather you from all over, and bring you back to your own land. I'll pour pure water over you and scrub you clean. I'll give you a new heart, put a new spirit in you. I'll remove the stone heart from your body and replace it with a heart that's God-willed, not self-willed. I'll put my Spirit in you and make it possible for you to do what I tell you and live by my commands. You'll once again live

in the land I gave your ancestors. You'll be my people! I'll be your
God! (Ezek. 36:24–28 THE MESSAGE)

Please note the active agent in this rescue mission. God! God will
rescue. God will gather. God will cleanse. He will give the people a
new heart, and, most important, he will put his Spirit in them, and as
a result they will obey God's commands.

Do you find this to be a stunning assurance? So did Ezekiel.
Consequently a field trip was in order.

GOD'S Spirit took me up and set me down in the middle of an open
plain strewn with bones. He led me around and among them—a lot
of bones! There were bones all over the plain—dry bones, bleached
by the sun. (37:1–2 THE MESSAGE)

Death Valley. No life to be found. No children playing, sweet-
hearts kissing, musicians singing, or dancers dancing. Only bones.
Dry bones.

God asked him, "Son of man, can these bones live?" (v. 3).

What a question.

I've never been to the valley that Ezekiel visited. But I sat next to a
person on a flight who told me that his life had lost all meaning. I've
never walked the valley of dry bones, but I've listened to a suicidal
mother describe a dark place from which she could find no exit. I've
never stepped through a field of femurs and rib cages, but I have spoken to a young man whose life was rubbed raw by opioid addiction.
I've not gazed at acres of fleshless forms, but I've witnessed the proud
left wordless at a funeral, not knowing what to say at the unwelcome
reminder of death. I've not found myself ankle deep in dry bones, but
I've looked in the mirror and seen a pastor with a dry faith and wondered if this hard heart could ever soften again.

Can these bones live?

The prophet was a man of vision. But not enough vision to venture an answer. He deferred. "Sovereign LORD, you alone know" (v. 3 NIV). Then the Lord gave this command:

Then he said to me, "Prophesy over these bones, and say to them, O dry bones, hear the word of the LORD. Thus says the Lord GOD to these bones: Behold, I will cause breath to enter you, and you shall live. And I will lay sinews upon you, and will cause flesh to come upon you, and cover you with skin, and put breath in you, and you shall live, and you shall know that I am the LORD." (vv. 4–6)

The prophet did as told. As he prophesied, Ezekiel heard a grand rattling. Bones clicked and clattered and reconnected. Sinew appeared out of nowhere to hinge the joints. Skin spread and refleshed the skeletons. The ravine of bones became a collection of bodies. Yet the bodies had no breath. No life. There was no evidence of beating hearts or breathing lungs. So God told the prophet to let loose another proclamation.

Then he said to me, "Prophesy to the breath; prophesy, son of man, and say to the breath, Thus says the LORD GOD: Come from the four winds, O breath, and breathe on these slain, that they may live." So I prophesied as he commanded me, and the breath came into them, and they lived and stood on their feet, an exceedingly great army. (vv. 9–10)

Apart from the Spirit we may have bones, flesh, scalps, and teeth, but we have no life. He, and he alone, is the giver of life. Lest we miss the message, God delivers the punch line. "And I will put my Spirit within you, and you shall live, and I will place you in your own land. Then you shall know that I am the LORD; I have spoken, and I will do it, declares the LORD" (v. 14).

God kept his promise. The Hebrews returned to their home-land some seventy years later. And they will return again in the new kingdom.

What the Spirit did then, he will do again for you.

"It is the Spirit who gives life; the flesh is no help at all" (John 6:63). This emptiness you feel? This zombiness? It won't be healed by a new house, spouse, job, or jewelry. A different date or weight might feel good, but the deep, lasting change you need? Only the Spirit can give it.

And he will!

Dry marriage? He can enliven it. Dead-end career? The Spirit can breathe on it. Scattered remnants of yesterday's dreams? The Spirit of God can reassemble and rekindle them. Do you feel as if you've been marched into Babylonian captivity? The Spirit can turn captives into an army.

It is not his will that you lead a lifeless life. He will breathe on your dry bones.

It simply falls on you to be an Ezekiel.

Surprised? "Me? Ezekiel?"

My invitation has nothing to do with changing your name, moving to Israel, or growing a belly-length beard. It has everything to do with your willingness to invite the Spirit into the dry and dead patches of your world.

The story of dry bones in Death Valley is so dramatic that we might miss a stunning element of this miracle. Ezekiel was invited to invite it. God told him to prophesy, and once he did—and only once he did—the wind of heaven began to blow.

What if the prophet had refused? What if he had declined? What if Ezekiel had heard the word and walked away, saying something like, "That's too supernatural for me." "I'm too small-time to be partner-ing with God." Or "He must have me confused with someone better, bigger, or holier."

But he didn't.

And you?

The breath of heaven is awaiting your invitation. Proclaim a declaration. State a heartfelt petition. *Spirit, I welcome you.*

He does not coerce, cajole, or force his way into our lives. He enters when welcomed, so for heaven's sake welcome him.

Does that seem too simple? It might. We tend to complicate this matter of receiving the Spirit. We create seven secrets of walking in the Spirit or ten requirements for receiving the Spirit or holy hints about the Holy Spirit. Yet the Spirit of God is not a computer to be programmed. He is a person to be welcomed.

Was this not the point Jesus made in the Upper Room?

It was the first Easter and, consequently, the first ever Easter worship service. Jesus rose from the dead that morning, and the disciples gathered in the Upper Room that evening. They had padlocked the door for fear that the leaders who came for Christ might come for them.

> The Spirit of God is not a computer to be programmed. He is a person to be welcomed.

"Then Jesus came and stood right in the middle of them and said, 'Peace be with you'" (John 20:19 NCV). We might expect Jesus to show exasperation at their trepidation. After all, angels had spoken. Rocks had broken. The ground had shaken like sloshing water. A covey of graves were suddenly tenantless. Someone ripped the temple veil in two, for crying out loud!

But the disciples? They were quivering like henless chicks.

Even so, Jesus showed up. They had locked the doors to stay safe, but no one is safe from the resurrected Lord. "Peace be with you," he said three times in this brief text (vv. 19, 21, 26). The first words of the risen Jesus to his apostles were words of comfort. Grace. Sheer grace.

His gift of peace was followed by a gift of power. "'As the Father sent me, I now send you.' After he said this, he breathed on them and said, 'Receive the Holy Spirit'" (vv. 21–22 NCV).

Jesus exhaled and they inhaled. He breathed on his disciples as God had breathed life into Adam (Gen. 2:7). I like the translation that reads: "[Jesus] breathed on them and said, 'Welcome the Holy Spirit!'" (John 20:22).[1]

No conditions. No prerequisites. No hoops to jump through or hurdles to jump over. No, Jesus gave his Spirit as he had given himself on the cross: as a gift, pure and undeserved. Paul's question to the Galatians is the question for us all: "Did you receive the Spirit by the works of the law, or by the hearing of faith?" (Gal. 3:2 NKJV).

The answer? Faith! Faith alone. Faith in Christ is the receptacle of the Spirit. The gospel never says, "Clean yourself up so God may come in." It offers, "Welcome Christ, and the Spirit will clean you up."

The question is often asked: Does a person need a second blessing, a post-conversion experience with the Holy Spirit in order to receive the power from on high? My answer is, "Yes! And not only a second but a third and a tenth and a thousandth!" I believe I received a fresh anointing of the Spirit this morning before I began working on this chapter.

Let us eagerly wait for the promised Holy Spirit, moment by moment, day by day. Let us hear again the command of Christ: receive the Holy Spirit. Whether he comes in the form of a gentle breath as he did on the first Easter, or a roaring wind as he did on Pentecost, let us receive him. But let us guard against a complex set of requirements that discourage and hinder the willing heart. The Spirit, like salvation, is received by simple faith.

You need not strive to earn what the Father is so happy to give. The winsome words of Jesus come to mind: "You fathers—if your children ask for a fish, do you give them a snake instead? Or if they ask for an egg, do you give them a scorpion? Of course not!" (Luke 11:11–12 NLT).

How absurd! No father would play such cruel tricks on his children. The youngster asks for a snack, and the dad says, "Sure, close your eyes and hold out your hand," and then places a poisonous spider on the child's palm? If any mother or father would do such a thing, they should not be parents.

"So if you sinful people know how to give good gifts to your children, how much more will your heavenly Father give the Holy Spirit to those who ask him" (Luke 11:13 NLT). If we, with our propensity toward self-centeredness, love our kids enough to keep them from evil and give them what is good, how much more would God do the same? And in his economy the ultimate good is the Holy Spirit.

The help you need is here. Ask the Spirit to infuse you with his power. Throw open the door! Swing wide the gate! Stand on the threshold and say, "Come in!" Inhale the one Jesus exhales. Take a deep, refreshing breath of the power and presence of God. Do so now, then again, then again.

> Spirit of the living God, breathe.
> Breath of the highest heaven, breathe.
> Over this weary world,
>   into our ossified dreams,
>   upon our skeletal frames,
>   breathe, dear Spirit, so we will live.

I never received an update on the snoring grandpa. I can only wonder what the old Rumpelstiltskin thought when he awoke to the presence of a soggy cracker on his tongue and the taste of juice in his mouth.

Of course it's one thing to sleep through a Communion service in a convalescent home. It is something else entirely to sleep through communion with the Spirit of the living God.

Please don't make that mistake. Invite him to blow breath on your bones.

The help you need is
here. Ask the Spirit
to infuse you with his
power. Throw open
the door! Swing wide
the gate! Stand on
the threshold and say,
"Come in!"

Are you weary? Inhale him. Is stress mounting? Inhale him. Does fear threaten to suck you out to sea? Take a deep breath of life. Little by little, one breath after another. Soon, before you know it, you will have inhaled Life into your life.

Questions for Reflection

PREPARED BY ANDREA LUCADO

1

The Holy Who?

1. Scripture tells us the Trinity is made up of three figures: Father, Son, and Holy Spirit. How would you describe each one?

2. What is your understanding of the Holy Spirit? On what is your knowledge based—teaching by the church, personal study, or something else?
   - What were you taught about the Holy Spirit in church or by your faith leaders?
   - How did this teaching, or lack thereof, affect the way you view the Spirit today?
   - What role, if any, does the Holy Spirit play in your life?

3. Max describes the moment in high school when he first learned about the Holy Spirit. He was taught that "the Spirit is your life-giving friend, here to lead you home" (p. 5).
   - Do you agree with this description of the Spirit? Has he

proved to be a "life-giving friend" in your life? Give an example.

- What would you change or add to this description?

4. Jesus instructed his disciples not to begin their ministries until they received the Holy Spirit. As Luke 24:49 says, "Don't begin telling others yet—stay here in the city until the Holy Spirit comes and fills you with power from heaven" (TLB). What does this tell you about the importance of the Holy Spirit in our lives and ministries?

5. Fill in the blank: The Holy Spirit comes with _____ (p. 7).
- What kind of power does the Holy Spirit give us?
- If you have experienced the Holy Spirit's power, explain the circumstances and what happened.
- How did you know you were experiencing the power of the Spirit?
- How do you need the Spirit's power to work in your life right now?

6. Max describes three different relationships we can have with the Holy Spirit:
   a. the *show-offs*, who make the rest of us feel they are more in tune with the Spirit than we are,
   b. the *Spirit Patrol*, who try to limit and control the role of the Spirit in their lives,
   c. and the *healthy saints*, who are open to the Spirit and discerning of the Spirit's voice.
      – Which one do you identify with most, and why?
      – Have you ever known a Holy Spirit show-off? How did this person affect the way you felt about the Holy Spirit?

– Have you ever known someone who was part of the Spirit Patrol? How did this person affect the way you felt about the Holy Spirit?

– Examine your own relationship with the Holy Spirit. Have you ever been part of the show-off or Spirit Patrol groups?

7. The Bible uses several metaphors to describe the Holy Spirit:
   - The Holy Spirit is the ultimate *teacher* (John 14:26).
   - The Spirit is the *wind* of God (John 3:8).
   - He is our *intercessor* (Rom. 8:26).
   - He is the *seal of heaven* upon the saint (Eph. 1:13).
   - He descends on us like a *dove* (Matt. 3:16).
   - He *equips* us with spiritual gifts (1 Cor. 12:1–11).
   - He is the *river of living water*, who flows out of us (John 7:37–39).
     – Have you experienced the Holy Spirit in any of the ways just listed? If so, in what ways?
     – Which description of the Spirit are you most curious about, and why?
     – Which one, if any, spurs your skepticism? Why?

8. Max poses this question: "Is it your desire to know the Holy Spirit better and to nurture your relationship with him?" (p. 11). How would you answer that?
   - Why did you decide to read *Help Is Here*?
   - How do you feel about the idea that the Spirit led you to read this book and to participate in this study?

2

Come Alongside Me

The Spirit As a Teacher

1. What are the qualities of a good teacher?
   - Who is the best teacher you've had (in school, in church, or elsewhere)?
   - What traits made this person a good teacher? In particular how did the good teacher change your life?

2. The Greek word for the Holy Spirit used in John 14, 15, and 16 is *Paraclete* (Helper). What are the different ways this word can be translated, and what is their central message? (See p. 16.)

3. Read the following verses, and underline every descriptive word or phrase used for the Holy Spirit.

"I will ask the Father, and he will give you another Helper [*Paraclete*], to be with you forever, even the Spirit of truth, whom the world cannot receive, because it neither sees him nor knows him. You know him, for he dwells with you and will be in you. . . . The Helper [*Paraclete*] . . . whom the Father will send in my name, he will teach you all things and bring to your remembrance all that I have said to you." (John 14:16–17, 26)

"When the Helper [*Paraclete*] comes, whom I will send to you from the Father, the Spirit of truth, who proceeds from the Father, he will bear witness about me." (John 15:26)

"It is to your advantage that I go away, for if I do not go away, the Helper [*Paraclete*] will not come to you. But if I go, I will send him to you. And when he comes, he will convict the world concerning sin and righteousness and judgment." (John 16:7–8)

"When the Spirit of truth comes, he will guide you into all the truth, for he will not speak on his own authority, but whatever he hears he will speak, and he will declare to you the things that are to come. He will glorify me, for he will take what is mine and declare it to you." (John 16:13–14)

- What descriptions speak most personally to you? Explain.
- Do you think of the Spirit in the ways the Spirit is

described in these verses—as your teacher, as one who glorifies Jesus, as one who convicts people of sin, as the bearer of truth, etc.? Why or why not?

4. Max explains that according to Scripture the Holy Spirit is not an *it*. The Holy Spirit is a divine being. Why is this an important distinction?

5. Fill in the blank: "Yet the Spirit has a specific, overarching mission. His task is to teach us about _____" (p. 18).
   - Why do we need the Holy Spirit to teach us about this subject?
   - How does the Spirit teach us about this subject?
   - Have you ever learned something about Jesus from the Holy Spirit? If so, what did you learn, and what was that experience like?

6. What are you struggling with in your life that a day-to-day teacher could help you with?
   - Do you feel confident that the Holy Spirit will respond and give you the guidance and teaching you need? Why or why not?
   - Have you seen evidence of this in the past? If so, give an example.

7. Read the story of Peter and Cornelius in Acts 10.
   - What role did the Holy Spirit play in the story?
   - What did the Holy Spirit tell Peter in verses 19–20?
   - How did Peter respond?
   - What did Peter ultimately learn about God, Jesus, the Jews, and the Gentiles in this passage?
   - What does this story tell you about the significance of

the Holy Spirit in understanding Jesus' message and purpose?

8. Max refers to a stressful season he had early in his ministry, saying, "I was under the impression that I had to fix everyone's problems, shoulder everyone's burdens, and never grow weary in doing so" (p. 22).
   - Have you ever felt this way? Perhaps you feel this way now. What burdens are you shouldering?
   - What revelation did Max have regarding this weight of responsibility he felt?
   - What can you do to invite the Holy Spirit's help? How could you rely on the Holy Spirit to take care of the burden you are carrying right now?

3

Raise Your Sail

The Spirit As Wind

1. What is a rowboat type of faith? What is a sailboat type of faith? Explain the difference in the two.
   - Do you have a rowboat or sailboat type of faith right now? What makes you say so?
   - Where does your rowboat or sailboat mentality come from—the church you grew up in, a mentor, what you've read in the Bible, or an aspect of your personality? Explain your response.

2. Read the story of Nicodemus in John 3:1–15.
   - In verse 3 what does Jesus tell Nicodemus he must do in order to see the kingdom of God?
   - What do you think of Nicodemus's response in verse 4?

- According to verse 5, how does Jesus say we are born again?
- Jesus compares the Spirit to the wind in verse 8. Why do you think he used this metaphor in this particular passage?
- Nicodemus expressed confusion during his conversation with Jesus. Are you puzzled by anything in this passage? If so, what?
- Does this passage help you understand the Holy Spirit in a new way? Explain your answer.
- What does this conversation tell us about the Holy Spirit and his power in our lives?

3. Max quotes theologian Abraham Kuyper, who compared the Spirit to the wind in that the Spirit does not appear "in visible form; He never steps out from the intangible void. Hovering, undefined, incomprehensible, He remains a mystery. He is as the wind! We hear its sound, but can not tell whence it cometh and whither it goeth. Eye can not see Him, ear can not hear Him, much less the hand handle Him" (p. 33).
   - Why is this, as Max describes it, good news?
   - Have you ever experienced the Holy Spirit in this way, as something you could not see but you felt? If so, how did you know you were experiencing the Spirit?

4. Max says that because we are "born of the Spirit" (John 3:8), "we have his wind, his unseen power, within us. We host the mystery and majesty of God" (p. 34).
   - If you have a rowboat type of faith, how could this power from the Spirit help you let go of the spiritual work you are doing?
   - Perhaps you have a rowboat type of faith in just some

aspects of your life. If so, what are those areas, and how could you rely on the Spirit for strength in those areas instead of relying on your own power?

5. Fill in the blanks: "Nicodemus was fixated on the word ___. The Christian is fixated on the word ___" (p. 35).
   • What is "done" in the Christian faith? Do you really believe this? Why or why not?
   • Would your thoughts and actions suggest you believe this truth? Why or why not?

6. Even if you've been a believer for a long time, it's easy to slide back into the rowboat type of faith.
   • Why do you think this is the case?
   • What do you need to believe about the Spirit, Jesus, or God in order to have a sailboat type of faith?

7. Imagine that you do have a sailboat type of faith, one in which you rely wholly on the Spirit for all your needs and struggles. How would your daily life look different from the way it looks now?
   • How would you be different from the way you are now?
   • How would you view yourself differently?
   • How would you view others differently?

8. Pinpoint one struggle you are facing today.
   • What would you do if you were rowing your boat through that struggle?
   • What would you do if you were sailing your way through that struggle?
   • In what way do you need to rely on the Spirit today to get through this struggle?

4

Groans of the Heart

The Spirit As Intercessor

1. What role does prayer have in your life? Do you pray often? Sometimes? Rarely? Do you keep a prayer list or journal? Why or why not?
   - Have you ever felt at a loss for words when praying? Why was it hard to find words during this prayer time?
   - What do you do when you don't know what to pray for?
   - Max says when we don't know what to pray for, our prayers are like "groans of the heart" (p. 42). Have you

ever felt as if your prayers were simply groans from
the heart rather than actual words? If so, what kind of
situation were you in?

- Was prayer—even with a lack of words—helpful during
this time? Why or why not?

2. Read Romans 8:22–23, 26–27:

"We know that the whole creation has been groaning as in
the pains of childbirth right up to the present time. Not only so,
but we ourselves, who have the firstfruits of the Spirit, groan
inwardly as we wait eagerly for our adoption to sonship, the
redemption of our bodies. . . . The Spirit helps us in our weakness. We do not know what we ought to pray for, but the Spirit
himself intercedes for us through wordless groans. And he who
searches our hearts knows the mind of the Spirit, because the
Spirit intercedes for God's people in accordance with the will
of God" (NIV).

- According to this passage in the context of prayer, what
does the Spirit do for us, and when?

- Have you ever thought about the Spirit interceding
for you in prayer? How does this idea make you feel?
Hopeful? Confused? Skeptical? Why?

3. Max points out that the word Paul used in Romans 8:26 for
weakness is the same word he used elsewhere in Scripture to
describe physical illness. Have you or someone you know ever
been sick to the point you didn't even know what to pray for?
Healing? Doctors? Medicine? A miracle? What was it like to
pray during that difficult time?

- Perhaps you haven't been physically sick to this degree
but you've had seasons of weakness because of losing
a job, losing someone you love, or going through a

divorce. Max describes it as a time when there is "a gap between what we want from life and what we get in life" (p. 44). What did you pray for during this time?

- When you're weak, is it difficult to pray? Why or why not?

4. Do you ever feel pressure to pray for the "right" thing?
   - If so, where do you think this pressure comes from?
   - How does this pressure affect your prayer life?
   - How would it affect your prayer life if you trusted what Romans says: "The Spirit himself intercedes for us" (8:26)?

5. Max uses a story from his time in Brazil to illustrate how the Spirit intercedes for us. Has anyone ever advocated for you in the way Quenho advocated for Max? If so, who was it, and how did that person's intercession affect your situation?
   - How does knowing that the Spirit is interceding on your behalf make you feel about your prayers?
   - How could believing that the Spirit is interceding on your behalf change the way you pray?
   - What does the Spirit's intercession tell us about the character of God and how he feels about his children?
   - Have you ever experienced the peace of prayer when someone prayed over you?

6. The Message's wording of Romans 8:27–28 says, "[The Spirit] keeps us present before God. That's why we can be so sure that every detail in our lives of love for God is worked into something good."
   - What is the promise in this passage?

- Is there anything in your life right now that you can't find the words to express in prayer? If so, how could you apply this passage to that situation? What kind of hope could this promise bring you today?

5

A Sure Salvation

The Spirit As a Seal

1. Max shares a story of traveling to see his grandparents when he was a child. His dad stuck into his pocket a piece of paper that said, "This boy belongs to Jack and Thelma Lucado" (p. 52). If you had experienced such a trip as a child, whose names would have been written on your piece of paper? Who gave you a secure sense of belonging?
   - How did this feeling of belonging affect you as you were growing up?
   - If you did not grow up with a strong sense of belonging, how did that affect you?

- Why do you think it's important to have a secure sense of belonging to our family, friends, and community?

2. According to Ephesians 1:13 and 4:30, to whom do we belong?
   - What is the significance of the verb *sealed*?
   - Max defines sealing as the act that says, "This is mine, and this is protected" (p. 52). Do you feel that way about anything or anyone in your life? If so, what or who?
   - Considering this, what does it mean for God to have sealed you to himself with the Holy Spirit?

3. Read Romans 8:14–17:

   "For all who are led by the Spirit of God are children of God. So you have not received a spirit that makes you fearful slaves. Instead, you received God's Spirit when he adopted you as his own children. Now we call him, 'Abba, Father.' For his Spirit joins with our spirit to affirm that we are God's children. And since we are his children, we are his heirs" (NLT).
   - What spirit have we *not* received?
   - What spirit *have* we received?
   - When did we receive that spirit?
   - According to Roman law what happened when a child was adopted? (See p. 54.)
   - What does this mean for our relationship to God?
   - What does this tell you about who you are in Christ?

4. Max points out that God is referred to as father fifteen times in the Old Testament. In the New Testament, however, God is referred to as father more than two hundred times. Do you relate to God as your father? If not, how do you relate to or view God?

- How would it affect you if you thought of God as a good father?
- What role does the Spirit play in allowing us to relate to God as our father? (See Galatians 4:6–7 and Romans 5:5.)

5. Second Corinthians 1:21–22 says, "God affirms us, making us a sure thing in Christ, putting his Yes within us. By his Spirit he has stamped us with his eternal pledge—a sure beginning of what he is destined to complete" (THE MESSAGE). What does the Spirit do to our salvation?
   - At this point in your faith journey, do you feel confident in your salvation? Why or why not?
   - How could the promise of being sealed in the Spirit affect the way you feel about your salvation?
   - Max poses the question "Why is this security important?" (p. 57). How would you answer that?
   - How do you act when you feel insecure?
   - How do you act when you feel secure?
   - If you were completely secure in your salvation, would this change the way you act today, the way you feel about yourself, or the way you feel about others? If so, how?

6. First John 4:18 suggests that if we fear for our salvation, it is because we have not experienced God's perfect love: "If we are afraid, it is for fear of punishment, and this shows that we have not fully experienced his perfect love" (NLT).
   - Do you feel that you've experienced God's perfect love? If so, how do you know? If not, what type of love have you felt from God?
   - Max defines God's perfect love in this way: "God loves

you with a perfect love: perfect knowledge of your past mistakes, perfect knowledge of your future missteps, and, yet, is perfectly willing to love you despite both" (p. 58). When we don't experience God's perfect love, it's not because his love is not perfect. It's often because we are unwilling to accept it. Is it hard for you to accept God's perfect love? Why or why not?

• With what you've learned about the Spirit in this chapter, how could you let God love you in his perfect way today?

6

Calm This Chaos

The Spirit As a Dove

1. Fill in the blanks: "Anxiety is not a sign of _____. But anxiety does _____ us" (p. 64).
   - What is causing you anxiety right now?
   - How does your anxiety affect you spiritually, physically, and emotionally?

2. Genesis 1:2 says, "The earth was without form, and void; and darkness was on the face of the deep. And the Spirit of God was hovering over the face of the waters" (NKJV). What is the Holy Spirit's purpose in this passage?

- What is significant about the verb *hovering*?
- What was possible after the Spirit calmed the earth?

3. Have you ever thought of the Holy Spirit as a calming presence? Why or why not?
    - Have you ever known the calming of the Holy Spirit? If so, how would you explain that experience?
    - Was this peace of the Holy Spirit different from the peace you've experienced elsewhere in your life? If so, in what way?

4. All four Gospels record Jesus' baptism and the Holy Spirit descending on him like a dove. Imagine that scene.
    - What do you think the witnesses saw?
    - How do you think this demonstration of the Spirit made Jesus feel?
    - List the physical and personality characteristics you know about a dove: _____, _____, _____
    - What does this image tell us about the Spirit?

5. Max points out that the dove was a feminine symbol in biblical times and that the Hebrew word used for "Spirit" is a feminine word. What are some uniquely feminine or motherly characteristics?
    - What female in your life have you gone to for comfort?
    - What unique comfort did this person provide you?
    - Why is it important that the Spirit has these feminine and motherly qualities?
    - How do you feel about the imagery of the Holy Spirit as feminine or motherly? Is it helpful for you? Strange or new? Do you resist it? Explain your response.

6. How do you typically cope with anxiety?
   - Which coping mechanisms help, and why?
   - Which fall short, and why?

7. What coping mechanism does Max suggest for combating anxiety? (See p. 71.)
   - Have you ever used praise or worship to fight your anxiety? If so, what was that experience like?
   - In what ways are praise and worship comforting to us when we are weary with anxiety?
   - What role can the Holy Spirit play in fighting anxiety with praise and worship?

8. Think about a time you felt comforted either by the person in your answer to question five or by praise and worship. What aspect of this person or experience brought you a sense of peace?
   - How could you apply this type of comfort to the anxiety you are facing today?
   - Spend some time in prayer asking the Spirit for comfort. Pay attention to any comforting words or feelings of peace the Spirit may be offering.

7

How to Hear from God

The Spirit As a Pillar of
Cloud and of Fire

1. When was the last time you had to make a big decision? What were you trying to decide?
    - How did you ultimately make your decision? Did you spend time praying, talking to friends, listing pros and cons, or something else?
    - How did this decision process make you feel?
    - Are big decisions hard for you to make? Why or why not?

2. How did God guide the Israelites after they fled Egypt?

    -   The Israelites had just been through a traumatic experience. (You can read more about their story in the chapters leading up to Exodus 13.) How did they respond to God's guidance?
    -   Would you like to have a clear sign from God about each step you should take in life? Why or why not?
    -   Why do you think God doesn't lead us with fire and pillars of clouds anymore?

3. According to Isaiah 63:11–14 who was the pillar of cloud and pillar of fire? Why did the Israelites need this type of guidance?

4. Max says, "Who leads the children of God today? The Holy Spirit! We have what the Hebrews had minus the manna" (p. 77).

    -   Have you ever consciously involved the Holy Spirit in your decision-making process? Why or why not?
    -   If you have, did you sense the Holy Spirit's guidance? If so, how?

5. Read Romans 12:2:

    "Don't copy the behavior and customs of this world, but let God transform you into a new person by changing the way you think. Then you will learn to know God's will for you, which is good and pleasing and perfect" (NLT).

    -   What does this verse tell us to do in order to know God's will for us?
    -   What behaviors and customs of the world do you think Paul was referring to here?
    -   How can following these customs keep us from knowing God's will for us?

- Have you ever "followed the crowd" in a direction that led you to a bad place? If so, what were the consequences?
- Have you ever resisted the temptation to follow the crowd? If so, where did God lead you instead?

6. Max says, "If you want to hear from God, the first question you need to ask is not 'What should I do?' but 'Whom will I hear? Who has authority? Who calls the shots in my life?'"
   - Who calls the shots in your life right now?
   - Is this voice leading you where you think God wants you to go? Explain.

7. After Moses built the tabernacle as God instructed, Scripture says, "Then the cloud covered the tabernacle of meeting, and the glory of the LORD filled the tabernacle" (Ex. 40:34 NKJV).
   - Where did the Spirit of God dwell from this moment on?
   - Why do you think God did this for the Israelites?
   - What significance does this have for us?
   - Do you believe the Holy Spirit dwells in you? If so, how do you know? If not, why not?

8. When we are trying to discern God's will for our lives, Max says, "Go first to the verse. Go next to the voice" (p. 82).
   - How can Scripture help us in our decision-making?
   - Has Scripture ever helped you make a decision? If so, how?
   - What is the voice Max is referring to?
   - Are you able to hear this voice? If so, what is an example of a time this voice provided guidance for you in deciding what to do next?

- From what you learned in this chapter, what do you think the voice of the Spirit sounds like?
- What does it not sound like?
- Why is this distinction important?

8

Soul on Fire

The Spirit As a Flame

1. When you hear phrases like "on fire for the Lord" or "on fire with the Spirit," what do those phrases mean to you?
   - Have you ever felt this way in your spiritual life? If so, when?
   - If you haven't heard phrases like this before, what do you think of them? Are they strange or confusing? Do they resonate with you? Explain your answer.

2. In this chapter Max explains three ways the Holy Spirit is like fire. The first is a refiner's fire. As Malachi 3:2–3 says:

   "For He is like a refiner's fire
   And like launderers' soap.

He will sit as a refiner and a purifier of silver;

He will purify the sons of Levi,

And purge them as gold and silver,

That they may offer to the LORD

An offering in righteousness." (NKJV)

- According to this passage what does a refiner's fire do?
- What is the resulting material after a refiner's fire?

3. When you try to imagine the Holy Spirit as a refining
or purifying fire, do you feel peaceful or nervous or
anxious or fearful? Can you explain the reasons for your
response?

   - Have you ever experienced the purifying power of the
   Holy Spirit in your life? If so, how did the Spirit change
   you in this process?
   - Is there anything in your life that needs this work
   from the Spirit—a bad habit, a sin pattern, a toxic
   relationship?
   - How could you invite the Spirit to purify this area of
   your life?

4. Fill in the blank: "Victory over sin is the result of the
presence of _____ _____ within us" (p. 91).

   - What part does this play in our strategy to conquer the
   sin in our lives?
   - How do you typically try to address your sin?
   - Does this strategy work? Explain.
   - What is the difference between what Paul wrote in
   Romans 7 and Romans 8?
   - How could you use more Holy Spirit and less "I" when
   it comes to facing your sin?

5. The second way the Holy Spirit is like fire is in his energy. Max shares a story about a student who had lost his passion for his faith. What was the student's reason for losing his passion, according to his pastor?
   - What role has community played in your faith?
   - Have you ever gone through a season—or perhaps you are in one now—without a church or faith community? How did that affect your faith?

6. Hebrews 10:24–25 says, "Let us consider how to provoke one another to love and good deeds, not neglecting to meet together, as is the habit of some, but encouraging one another, and all the more as you see the Day approaching" (NRSV).
   - According to these verses how does community help refine us?
   - How does community encourage our faith?

7. Finally, the Holy Spirit is like fire in that he can protect us. God says in Zechariah 2:5, "I myself will be a wall of fire around it . . . and I will be its glory within" (NIV).
   - What do you need spiritual protection from? Sin, anxious thoughts, fears?
   - How does it feel to know you can be protected from these things by the fire of the Holy Spirit?

8. In what ways do you need the fire of the Holy Spirit today?
   - In what ways do you need the refining of the Holy Spirit?
   - In what ways do you need the energy of the Holy Spirit?
   - In what ways do you need the protection of the Spirit?

9. End your study time reflecting on David's words in Psalm 139. Pray that the Holy Spirit will see every part of you and do a mighty work.

> God, examine me and know my heart;
>> test me and know my anxious thoughts.
> See if there is any bad thing in me.
>> Lead me on the road to everlasting life. (vv. 23–24 NCV)

9

Oily Footprints

The Spirit As Anointing Oil

1. Have you ever been given a new title or a new role? Perhaps you were named to a new position at work or took on a new role in life such as "mother" or "uncle."
   - Think of a time you received a new assignment.
   - Was there any sort of ritual, ceremony, or celebration to mark this change? If so, why did you mark it in this way?
   - Why do you think cultures have rituals and celebrations to mark changes like these in our lives?

2. Read the following passages.

   "Samuel took the flask of olive oil he had brought and anointed David with the oil. And the Spirit of the LORD came powerfully upon David from that day on." (1 Sam. 16:13 NLT)

"Anoint Elisha son of Shaphat from the town of Abel-meholah to replace you as my prophet." (1 Kings 19:16 NLT)

"God . . . poured fragrant oil on your head, marking you out as king, far above your dear companions." (Heb. 1:9 THE MESSAGE)

"The Spirit of the Lord is upon me, because he has anointed me." (Luke 4:18)
- In these passages what role does oil play?
- What was the significance of anointing someone with oil?
- How is this ritual of anointing someone with oil similar to the ritual or celebration you talked about in question 1? How is it different?

3. According to 2 Corinthians 1:21–22, how has God anointed us?
   - Considering the passages in question 2, how does this anointing change our identity?
   - How do you feel about the imagery of being anointed with the Spirit? Is this a familiar or strange concept for you? Explain your response.

4. When Moses anointed Aaron and his sons, it marked their new identities as priests of the Lord. What does Max say was the significance of this? (See p. 100.)

5. First John 2:20 says we have a similar anointing to Aaron: "But you have an anointing from the Holy One [you have been set apart, specially gifted and prepared by the Holy Spirit], and all of you know [the truth because He teaches us, illuminates our minds, and guards us from error]" (AMP).

   - What does your anointing say about your purpose?
   - What does your anointing say about God's favor upon you?
   - What does your anointing say about your authority?

6. Acts 2:17 says, "And in the last days it shall be, God declares, that I will pour out my Spirit on all flesh." What is significant about the verb *pour*?

7. "You've been anointed by the Holy Spirit. This anointing changes everything," says Max (p. 102). Do you feel as though the Holy Spirit's anointing has changed you? If so, in what ways?

   - If you're unsure, how could the confidence of this anointing change the way you think and feel about yourself?
   - How could it change the way you relate to others?
   - How could it change the way you view your purpose in life?

8. Max shares a story of how the Holy Spirit's power intervened in a conversation he was having with a friend.

   - What did Max do during this conversation?
   - How did the Holy Spirit respond?
   - Has the Spirit ever intervened for you in this way— given you wisdom or knowledge you wouldn't have had otherwise? If so, what did the Spirit teach or show you?

9. What would your day look like if you consistently reminded yourself that you are anointed by the Holy Spirit, that the Spirit's power has been poured on you, and that you now walk with the Spirit's authority?

10

The Coming Wave

The Spirit As a River
of Living Water

1. Max describes the state of Christianity in America in the late eighteenth century. How does this spiritual landscape compare to the one you see around you today?
   - Is Christianity alive and well where you live, or is it dwindling in its influence?
   - How do you feel about the state of faith in your community?

2. How would you define *revival*?
    - Have you ever been a part of a revival or witnessed one? If so, what was it like for you or those who were a part of it?
    - Have you ever experienced a personal revival—a reviving of your own faith? If so, what prompted this revival for you?

3. Read John 7:37–39:

    On the last and most important day of the feast Jesus stood up and said in a loud voice, "Let anyone who is thirsty come to me and drink. If anyone believes in me, rivers of living water will flow out from that person's heart, as the Scripture says." Jesus was talking about the Holy Spirit. The Spirit had not yet been given, because Jesus had not yet been raised to glory. But later, those who believed in Jesus would receive the Spirit. (NCV)

    Jesus spoke these words at the end of the Feast of Tabernacles, which celebrated the miracle of the rock that gave water to Moses and his people. Read that story in Exodus 17:1–7.
    - What is the significance of Jesus' saying these words during a festival that commemorated this miracle?
    - If you had been in the crowd that day and were familiar with the miracle during Moses' time, what would you have thought of Jesus' words?
    - What does "living water" symbolize?

4. Max points out the significance of these words: "Let anyone who is thirsty come to me and drink" (v. 37).
    - According to this passage who is invited to come to Jesus and drink?

- What promise does this give you?
- Do you feel a spiritual thirst for anything in your life right now? If so, for what?
- How have you tried to quench this thirst?
- According to this passage whom should we go to in order to quench our thirst?
- In what ways can Jesus uniquely quench our spiritual thirst?

5. Next Jesus said, "If anyone believes in me, rivers of living water will flow out from that person's heart" (v. 38 NCV).
   - What did Jesus mean by this?
   - Max says when the Spirit flows out of Christ followers, "We refresh. We soothe. We soften. The Holy Spirit flows out of us into the dry places of the world" (p. 111). Has the Spirit ever worked through you in this way? If so, what was the result?
   - Or have you ever experienced the Spirit from someone else in this way? If so, how did the Spirit's flowing out of this person affect you?

6. Max says the Spirit flowing out of us can lead to revival (p. 113). What would it look like in your community or city if every Christ follower in that area allowed the Holy Spirit to flow out of them? What would change?
   - What prevents us from letting the Spirit flow out of us?
   - Can you imagine a Cane Ridge type of revival happening today in your city? Explain your answer.
   - What prayers do you have for your city?
   - What role could you play in making these prayers a reality for your community?

7. Max wrote a short prayer at the end of this chapter: *God, please release living water upon and through your children. Let us be sources of life and love everywhere we go. We want to be useful servants.* How could you be a source of life and love everywhere you go today?

11

Speak Up

The Spirit As Tongues of Fire

1. At the beginning of this chapter, we met a new Peter, one who was bold and preaching the good news during Pentecost. Read Acts 2:14, 38–39:

   Then Peter stood up with the Eleven, raised his voice and addressed the crowd: "Fellow Jews and all of you who live in Jerusalem, let me explain this to you; listen carefully to what I say. . . . Repent and be baptized, every one of you, in the name of Jesus Christ for the forgiveness of your sins. And you will receive the gift of the Holy Spirit. The promise is for you and your children and for all who are far off—for all whom the Lord our God will call." (NIV)

- What three things did Peter do in verse 14?
- How would you describe the tone of his words to the crowd?

2. Read what Peter did after Passover and before Jesus' crucifixion (Luke 22:54–62).
   - How would you describe Peter in this passage?
   - How does his behavior in Luke 22 compare to his behavior in Acts 2?
   - In your faith right now do you feel more like a Passover Peter or a Pentecost Peter? Why?

3. Do you know anyone who has a strong Pentecost faith like Peter's? If so, what qualities does this person have?
   - What makes this person's faith strong and courageous as Peter's was on that Pentecost?
   - How would you answer Max's question about Pentecost Peter: "What's gotten into Peter?" (p. 117).

4. Read Acts 2:2–6:

> Suddenly a sound like the blowing of a violent wind came from heaven and filled the whole house where they were sitting. They saw what seemed to be tongues of fire that separated and came to rest on each of them. All of them were filled with the Holy Spirit and began to speak in other tongues as the Spirit enabled them.
>
> Now there were staying in Jerusalem God-fearing Jews from every nation under heaven. When they heard this sound, a crowd came together in bewilderment, because each one heard their own language being spoken. (NIV)

- How did the Spirit arrive?
- What did the Spirit look like?
- Whom did the Spirit fill?
- What did the Spirit enable the people who were gathered that day to do?
- Why is it significant that this act of the Spirit occurred in Jerusalem on Pentecost?
- How many nations were represented in the house that day?
- What does this story tell you about the power of the Holy Spirit?
- What does it tell you about those the Spirit can work through?

5. In Acts 2:12 witnesses of this event of the Spirit asked, "Whatever could this mean?" (NKJV). How would you answer this question?

6. Have you ever felt at a loss for words when sharing your faith? Or have you ever regretted not speaking up about your faith?
   - If so, what kept you silent, or why was it difficult to find the words you wanted to say?
   - What does the story of Pentecost tell us about sharing our faith with others?
   - Who has shared their faith with you?
   - What words did they use?
   - What do you think made them able to share their belief with you?

7. Max shares the stories of three ordinary people who experienced profound conversions that they then shared with others: Brenda Jones, Antenor Goncalves (and his father), and

Max's high school friend Mike. Of these three stories which one resonated with you the most, and why?

- What did all three people have in common?
- How did they share their faith experiences in different ways?
- What impact did their sharing have on others?
- What does this tell you about the different ways the Spirit can use us to share God with our neighbors?
- How could the Spirit use you? Do you like to share your faith with people one-on-one like Brenda, by preaching like Antenor, or through your actions like Mike?

8. What is an Ebenezer?
   - Do you have any Ebenezers in your life? If so, what are they, and why are these significant moments for you?
   - Do you feel called to share your story of faith with someone in your life or through the work of writing or teaching? If you do, with whom do you want to share your story, and how could you tell this person or group of people about your Ebenezer?
   - If you are hesitant to share your faith story, how could this Ebenezer embolden you to do so?

12

You Unleashed

The Spirit As the
Gift Giver

1. What did you know about spiritual gifts before reading this chapter?
   - Do you have any spiritual gifts? If so, what are they, and when did you realize these were gifts?
   - If you're not very familiar with the idea of spiritual gifts, is this something you'd like to explore? What questions do you have?

2. Max references five passages that list gifts of the Spirit: 1 Corinthians 12:8–10; 1 Corinthians 12:28–30; Romans 12:6–8; Ephesians 4:11–12; and 1 Peter 4:10–11. Read these passages, and list every gift they mention.
    • How many different gifts of the Spirit do you find here?
    • Which gifts on these lists do you think you have?
    • Do you consider some gifts more important than others? If so, which ones, and why?

3. Fill in the blanks: "The presence of gifts requires the _____ to use them _____" (p. 133).
    • How could someone use a spiritual gift in an unwise or immature way?
    • Have you or someone you know ever misused a spiritual gift? If so, what was the result?
    • What is the danger of misusing a spiritual gift?

4. What is the difference between a natural talent and a spiritual gift?
    • What are some of your natural talents?
    • What are your spiritual gifts?
    • Do you use any of your natural talents for God's purpose? If so, how? If not, can you imagine a way to do this?

5. What are the discerning gifts?
    • Do you or someone you know have one of these gifts?
    • If you have a discerning gift, how has this gift been helpful in your spiritual life?
    • Or if you've encountered someone with a discerning gift, has that person's gift blessed your spiritual journey? If so, how?

6. What are the dynamic gifts?
   - Do you or someone you know have one of these gifts?
   - If you have a dynamic gift, how has this gift been helpful in your spiritual life?
   - Or if you've encountered someone with a dynamic gift, have that person's gifts blessed your spiritual journey? If so, how?

7. What are the declarative gifts?
   - Do you or someone you know have one of these gifts?
   - If you have a declarative gift, how has this gift been helpful in your spiritual life?
   - Or if you've ever encountered someone with a declarative gift, have that person's gifts blessed your spiritual journey? If so, how?

8. Max shares his story of receiving the gift of speaking in tongues despite having mixed feelings and thoughts about this gift at times in his ministry. Are you hesitant about or skeptical of any gifts? If so, which ones, and why?
   - Has what you learned in this chapter affected or changed those hesitations? If so, how?
   - Perhaps you have a long history with or a deep belief in spiritual gifts. If so, how has this chapter encouraged you in that part of your spiritual journey?

9. Max quotes a professor of theology who talked about little-godders and big-godders.
   - What is a little-godder?
   - What is a big-godder?
   - Considering the state of your faith today, would you consider yourself a little-godder or a big-godder, and why?

10. Answer the two questions Max poses toward the end of this chapter:

    - What would happen if each believer identified and employed his or her Spirit-given gifts?
    - What if each of us operated according to the prompting and provision of the Spirit?

13

Breath on Bones

The Spirit As Breath

1. In this chapter Max talks about the vision of the dry bones in Ezekiel 37. Read the passage below:

> "God's Spirit took me up and set me down in the middle of an open plain strewn with bones. He led me around and among them—a lot of bones! There were bones all over the plain—dry bones, bleached by the sun." (vv. 1–2 THE MESSAGE)

- Ezekiel saw dry bones and felt hopeless. Are there any "dry bones" in your life that give you a sense of hopelessness? What are they?
- Strikingly, God invited Ezekiel to invite his Spirit. How does he do the same with you?

2. Read Ezekiel 37:4–6:

> Then he said to me, "Prophesy over these bones, and say to them, O dry bones, hear the word of the LORD. Thus says the Lord GOD to these bones: Behold, I will cause breath to enter you, and you shall live. And I will lay sinews upon you, and will cause flesh to come upon you, and cover you with skin, and put breath in you, and you shall live, and you shall know that I am the LORD."

Read verses 7–8:

> So I prophesied as I was commanded. And as I prophesied, there was a sound, and behold, a rattling, and the bones came together, bone to its bone. And I looked, and behold, there were sinews on them, and flesh had come upon them, and skin had covered them. But there was no breath in them.

- What happened to the dry bones when Ezekiel prophesied over them?
- What didn't happen to the bones?

3. Read Ezekiel 37:9–10:

> Then he said to me, "Prophesy to the breath; prophesy, son of man, and say to the breath, Thus says the Lord

God: Come from the four winds, O breath, and breathe on these slain, that they may live." So I prophesied as he commanded me, and the breath came into them, and they lived and stood on their feet, an exceedingly great army.

- What happened to the bodies when Ezekiel prophesied to the breath?
- What does the breath represent?
- Where did the breath come from?
- What role does breath play in our bodies?
- What does this tell you about the vital nature of the Holy Spirit?

4. What role did Ezekiel play in bringing the dry bones back to life? What does this tell you about the role we play in bringing our dry bones back to life?

5. Read John 20:19–23:

On the evening of that day, the first day of the week, the doors being locked where the disciples were for fear of the Jews, Jesus came and stood among them and said to them, "Peace be with you." When he had said this, he showed them his hands and his side. Then the disciples were glad when they saw the Lord. Jesus said to them again, "Peace be with you. As the Father has sent me, even so I am sending you." And when he had said this, he breathed on them and said to them, "Receive the Holy Spirit. If you forgive the sins of any, they are forgiven them; if you withhold forgiveness from any, it is withheld."

- How did Jesus give the disciples the Holy Spirit?
- What is significant about how Jesus gave the disciples the Spirit?
- What does this tell you about how and when God will give you his Spirit?
- Have you allowed God to give you his Spirit as a gift? Why or why not?
- If you have, how have you experienced the Spirit as a gift?
- If you haven't, what is holding you back from receiving the Spirit?

6. Think about the dry parts of your life you talked about in question one. What would those dry bones look like if they were to come to life?
    - Have you asked the Spirit to breathe on these dry areas of your life? Why or why not?
    - Imagine your dry "bones" reviving and becoming vibrant. How would your life be different by partnering with the Spirit in this way?

7. Perhaps you are the one who feels dry. As Max says, "Are you weary? Inhale him. Is stress mounting? Inhale him. Does fear threaten to suck you out to sea? Take a deep breath of life" (p. 155). Take a deep breath right now. As you do, ask the Holy Spirit to breathe life into every dry bone in your body, and trust that the Spirit can give you new life.

Notes

Acknowledgments

1. Bernard L. Ramm, *Rapping about the Spirit* (Waco, TX: Word, 1974), 7. On the matter of the difficulties in studying the Holy Spirit, see also Millard J. Erickson, *Christian Theology*, unabridged, one-volume ed. (Grand Rapids: Baker Books, 1983), 846–48.

Chapter 1: The Holy Who?

1. Is the Holy Spirit a he? A she? The answer is neither. The Holy Spirit did not take on human form. No gender applies to the third member of the Trinity. The word *spirit* is both male and female in Hebrew, neuter in Greek, and only becomes male in Latin. Many writers find it helpful to avoid gender references altogether and only refer to the Spirit as "the Spirit." For the ease of reading and to follow the example of Jesus in John 14–16, I occasionally refer to the Spirit as "he." (I initially attempted to rotate between "he" and "she" but found that approach to be jarring.) To be clear, however, the Spirit is beyond our gender limitations. I trust the reader will keep that in mind and the Spirit will bring that truth to our minds as needed.

2. Comforts (Acts 9:31). Directs (Acts 13:2, 4; 15:28; 21:11). Indwells, transforms, sustains, and will someday deliver us into our heavenly home (Rom. 14:17; 15:13; 1 Cor. 12:3; 2 Cor. 3:17–18; Jude 20–21).

Chapter 2: Come Alongside Me

1. The fifth occasion is 1 John 2:1.
2. Lifeway Research, *2018 State of American Theology Study, Research Report,* http://lifewayresearch.com/wp-content/uploads/2018/10 /Ligonier-State-of-Theology-2018-White-Paper.pdf, p. 3.
3. J. I. Packer, *Keep in Step with the Spirit: Finding Fullness in Our Walk with God,* rev. ed. (Grand Rapids: Baker Books, 2005), 57, emphasis in the original.
4. Frederick Dale Bruner, *The Gospel of John: A Commentary* (Grand Rapids, MI: Eerdmans, 2012), 867.
5. Packer, *Keep in Step,* 212–13.

Chapter 3: Raise Your Sail

1. "Katie Spotz," Wikipedia, https://en.wikipedia.org/wiki/Katie_Spotz; Christopher Maag, "Woman Is the Youngest to Cross an Ocean Alone," *New York Times,* March 14, 2010, https://www.nytimes.com /2010/03/15/sports/15row.html.
2. "Laura Dekker," Wikipedia, https://en.wikipedia.org/wiki/Laura_Dekker.
3. This story came from Bill Frey, a friend.
4. "The work of salvation never started with the efforts of any man. God the Holy Spirit must begin it. Now, the reasons no man ever started the work of grace in his own heart are very apparent: first, because he cannot; second, because he won't. The best reason of all is because he cannot; he is dead. The dead may be made alive, but the dead cannot make themselves alive, for the dead can do nothing." Charles Spurgeon, *Spurgeon on the Holy Spirit* (New Kensington, PA: Whitaker, 2000), 16.
5. Abraham Kuyper, *The Work of the Holy Spirit,* trans. Henri de Vries (London: Funk & Wagnalls, 1900), 6.

Chapter 4: Groans of the Heart

1. Jurgen Moltmann, *The Spirit of Life: A Universal Affirmation* (Minneapolis, MN: Fortress, 1992), 51, as quoted by Leonard Allen, *Poured Out: The Spirit of God Empowering the Mission of God* (Abilene, TX: Abilene Christian University, 2018), 164.
2. "The Full Story of Thailand's Extraordinary Cave Rescue," BBC News,

14 July 2018, https://www.bbc.com/news/world-asia-44791998. "Tham Luang Cave Rescue," Wikipedia, https://en.wikipedia.org/wiki/Tham _Luang_cave_rescue#:~:text=The%20rescue%20effort%20involved %20over,pumping%20of%20more%20than%20a.

Chapter 5: A Sure Salvation

1. "An owner seals his property with his signet to mark it as his; if at a later time he comes to claim it and his right to it is questioned, his seal is sufficient evidence and puts an end to such questioning. So, the fact that believers are endowed with the Spirit is the token that they belong in a special sense to God. . . . Other seals, literal or figurative (like circumcision, the seal of the covenant with Abraham), were affixed externally; the seal of the new covenant is imprinted in the believing heart." (F. F. Bruce, *The Epistle to the Ephesians: A Verse-by-Verse Exposition* [London: Revell, 1961], 36).

2. George V. Wigram and Ralph D. Winter, *The Word Study Concordance* (Wheaton, IL: Tyndale, 1978), 715, note 4973.

3. Robert H. Stein, "Fatherhood of God," *Baker's Evangelical Dictionary of Biblical Theology,* http://www.biblestudytools.com /dictionaries/bakers-evangelical-dictionary/fatherhood-of-god.html.

4. Spiros Zodhiates, ed., *Hebrew-Greek Key Word Study Bible: Key Insights into God's Word*, New International Version (Chattanooga, TN: AMG Publishers, 1996), 2023, #8959.

5. "The Spirit Confirms Our Adoption," Grace to You, May 29, 1983, http://www.gty.org/resources/sermons/45-59/the-spirit-confirms-our -adoption?term=adoption.

6. Ada Habershon, "He Will Hold Me Fast," https://www.google.com /search?q=he+will+hold+me+fast+ada+habershon+shane+and+shane+ yrics&oq=He+will+hold+me+fast&aqs=chrome.0.69i59l3j46j0j69i60l3 .11279j0j7&sourceid=chrome&ie=UTF-8.

7. Robert Robinson, "Come Thou Fount of Every Blessing," Indelible Grace Hymn Book, http://hymnbook.igracemusic.com/hymns/come -thou-fount-of-every-blessing. Public Domain.

8. "COVID-19 Patient Writes Inspiring Message on Glass to Caregivers," Cleveland Clinic, March 28, 2020, YouTube, https://www.youtube .com/watch?v=pIzNAgiBETM.

Chapter 6: Calm This Chaos

1. "Svalbard Global Seed Vault," Crop Trust, www.croptrust.org/our -work/svalbard-global-seed-vault/.

2. Dorothy Willette, "The Enduring Symbolism of Doves: From Ancient Icon to Biblical Mainstay," Biblical Archaeology Society, August 5, 2021, https://www.biblicalarchaeology.org/daily/ancient-cultures/daily -life-and-practice/the-enduring-symbolism-of-doves/.

3. "Application of Science: Only Mammals Make Milk, Right?" Irish Examiner, April 12, 2021, https://www.irishexaminer.com/lifestyle /healthandwellbeing/arid-40262018.html.

4. "Americans Say They Are More Anxious; Baby Boomers Report Greatest Increase in Anxiety," American Psychiatric Association, May 6, 2018, https://www.psychiatry.org/newsroom/news -releases/americans-say-they-are-more-anxious-than-a-year-ago-baby -boomers-report-greatest-increase-in-anxiety#:~:text=New%20 York%20%E2%80%93%20Americans'%20anxiety%20 levels,%2C%20finances%2C%20relationships%20and%20politics. "This year's national anxiety score—derived by mean scores on a 0-100 scale, is 51, a five-point jump since 2017. Increases in anxiety scores were seen across age groups, across people of different race/ ethnicity and among men and women. By generation, millennials continued to be more anxious than Gen Xers or baby boomers, but baby boomers' anxiety increased the most with a seven-point jump between 2017 and 2018."

5. Amplified Bible, Classic Edition.

Chapter 7: How to Hear from God

1. Associated Press, "450 Turkish Sheep Leap to Their Deaths," FoxNews, July 8, 2005, https://www.foxnews.com/story/450-turkish -sheep-leap-to-their-deaths, updated January 13, 2015.

Chapter 8: Soul on Fire

1. Sebastian Junger, Fire (New York: Norton, 2002), 43.

2. "The Good and Bad of Forest Fires," My Land Plan, American Forest Foundation, https://mylandplan.org/content/good-and-bad -forest-fires.

3. J. D. Greear, Jesus, Continued . . . : Why the Spirit Inside You Is Better Than Jesus Beside You (Grand Rapids: Zondervan, 2014), 26. The numbers will vary slightly in the various Bible versions.

4. Anne Graham Lotz, Jesus in Me: Experiencing the Holy Spirit As a Constant Companion (Colorado Springs, CO: Multnomah, 2019), 132–33.

Chapter 9: Oily Footprints

1. William R. Moody, *The Life of Dwight L. Moody* (New York: Revell, 1900), 149.

Chapter 10: The Coming Wave

1. Mark Galli, "Revival at Cane Ridge, Christian History Institute, https://christianhistoryinstitute.org/magazine/article/revival-at-cane-ridge.
2. Paul Conkin, quoted in Galli, "Revival at Cane Ridge."
3. "Mark Galli: Why Aren't Evangelicals Obeying Jesus in Communion & Baptism?" Black Christian News Network, July 10, 2019, https://blackchristiannews.com/2019/07/mark-galli-why-arent-evangelicals-obeying-jesus-in-communion-baptism/.
4. "Second Great Awakening," Ohio History Central, https://ohiohistorycentral.org/w/Second_Great_Awakening.
5. "In U. S., Decline of Christianity Continues at Rapid Pace," Pew Research Center, October 17, 2019, https://www.pewforum.org/2019/10/17/in-u-s-decline-of-christianity-continues-at-rapid-pace/.
6. Adam Hadhazy, "Twenty Startling Facts about American Society and Culture," Live Science, July 6, 2015, https://www.livescience.com/51448-startling-facts-about-american-culture.html.
7. Brian Resnick, "22 Percent of Millennials Say They Have 'No Friends,'" VOX, August 1, 2019, https://www.vox.com/science-and-health/2019/8/1/20750047/millennials-poll-loneliness.
8. Maggie Fox, "Major Depression on the Rise Among Everyone, New Data Shows," NBC News, May 11, 2018, https://www.nbcnews.com/health/health-news/major-depression-rise-among-everyone-new-data-shows-n873146.
9. Jamie Ducharme, "U.S. Suicide Rates Are the Highest They've Been Since World War II," Time, June, 20, 2019, https://time.com/5609124/us-suicide-rate-increase/.
10. James Montgomery Boice, *The Gospel of John: An Expositional Commentary, Five Volumes in One* (Grand Rapids: Zondervan, 1985), 499.
11. John 7:37 NASB, emphasis added.
12. C. S. Lewis, *The Silver Chair* (New York: Macmillan, 1953), 16–17.
13. Conrad Hackett and David McClendon, "Christians Remain World's Largest Religious Group, but They Are Declining in Europe," Pew Research, April 5, 2017, https://www.pewresearch.org/fact-tank

/2017/04/05/christians-remain-worlds-largest-religious-group-but-they
-are-declining-in-europe/.

14. Stephen F. Olford, *Heart Cry for Revival* (Memphis, TN: Olford Ministries, 2005), 18.

15. James Burns, *Revivals: Their Laws and Leaders* (London: Hodder and Stoughton, 1909),19.

16. Jonathan Edwards, quoted in J. D. Greear, *Jesus, Continued* (Grand Rapids: Zondervan, 2014), 195.

17. Roy Jenkins, "The Welsh Revival," BBC, June 16, 2009, https://www .bbc.co.uk/religion/religions/christianity/history/welshrevival_1.shtml.

18. "1904 Revival," Moriah Chapel, www.moriahchapel.org.uk/index .php?page=1904-revival.

Chapter 11: Speak Up

1. A different Judas from the one who betrayed Christ.

2. *The Book of Acts in Its First Century Setting*, ed. Richard Bauckham, vol. 4, *The Book of Acts in Its Palestinian Setting* (Grand Rapids: Eerdmans, 1995), 260.

3. "For God so loved the world that he gave his one and only Son, that whoever believes in him shall not perish but have eternal life" (John 3:16 NIV).

4. Robert P. Menzies, *Empowered for Witness: The Spirit in Luke–Acts* (London: T&T International, 2004), 258.

5. Matthew 28:19–20 NIV.

6. This story is used with permission from Samuel Justin's son, Rev. Linus Samuel Justin.

Chapter 12: You Unleashed

1. Appreciation to Robert Morris for suggesting this manner of outlining the gifts of the Spirit. See *The God I Never Knew: How Real Friendship with the Holy Spirit Can Change Your Life* (Colorado Springs, CO: WaterBrook, 2011), 124–44.

2. Donald Barnhouse, *Romans*, quoted in Charles R. Swindoll, *The Tale of the Tardy Oxcart and 1,501 Other Stories* (Nashville: Word Publishing, 1998), 233.

Chapter 13: Breath on Bones

1. Frederick Dale Bruner, *The Gospel of John: A Commentary* (Grand Rapids: Eerdmans, 2012), 1164.

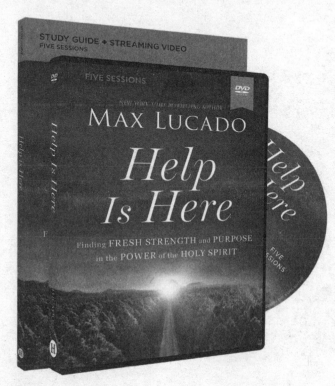

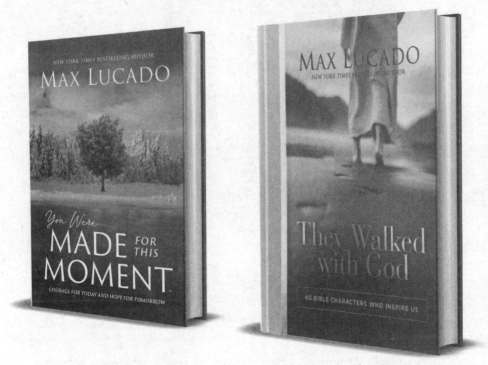

MAX LUCADO
BESTSELLERS

Anxious for Nothing

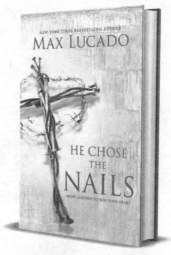

He Chose the Nails

Facing Your Giants

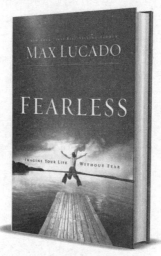

Fearless

WWW.MAXLUCADO.COM

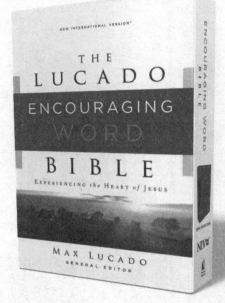

Inspired by what you just read?
Connect with Max.

Listen to Max's teaching ministry, UpWords, on the radio and online. Visit www.MaxLucado.com to get FREE resources for spiritual growth and encouragement, including:

- Archives of *UpWords*, Max's daily radio program, and a list of radio stations where it airs
- Devotionals and e-mails from Max
- First look at book excerpts
- Downloads of audio, video, and printed material
- Mobile content

You will also find an online store and special offers.

www.MaxLucado.com

1-800-822-9673

UpWords Ministries
P.O. Box 692170
San Antonio, TX 78269-2170